The
Graceful Art of Tea

Nan Taylor

Tea Time Blessings
Nan Taylor

The Graceful Art of Tea
Nan Taylor

Copyright © 2003 Taylor-Brown Publishing
All rights reserved.

Scripture taken from the New American Standard Bible
© 1960, 1962, 1963, 1971, 1972, 1973, 1975, 1977, 1995
by The Lockman Foundation. Used by permission.

Cover painting "A Tea Party in the Garden" by Alfred Oliver used by
permission of the Fine Art Photographic Library, London, England.

Design: Charles Logston
Illustrations: Scott Heming
Photography: Kory Washburn
Children's Tea Party Girls:
Alec & Jordyn Bender, and Cari Logston

ISBN 0-9743707-0-3

Printed in the United States of America

Taylor-Brown Publishing
PO Box 2954
Santa Clarita, CA 91386-2954
www.teagraces.com

Second Printing, 2005

I affectionately dedicate this book to my
three precious granddaughters:

Alec, Jordyn, and Tia

May you enjoy many years
of tipping the teacup!

Acknowledgements

$\mathcal{I}$ express my deep gratitude for the time and effort the following people have put into helping me see my dream come true.

My heartfelt thanks to Kory Washburn who had a vision of completeness and went above and beyond to help me get this book published.

Charles Logston used his creative expertise in the design and production. He worked with me patiently and tirelessly. Many, many thanks!

Scott Heming did a fabulous job with the illustrations considering he is a guy and doesn't really set tea tables or make tea sandwiches.

With patience and encouragement, my sweet friend Lenore Stein spent many hours editing and re-editing this manuscript.

Joyce Modert and Viki Bossom worked with me on several difficult sections revising and editing to make this book the best it could be.

My warm appreciation to Sheryl Ann Crawford and Elizabeth George for their endorsement of this book and their assurance and support from its inception.

Nina McGlamery, Joy Collette, Christine Kingsland, Gloria Landman, Wanda Wilson, my sweet daughter Dulcie Bender, and many other ladies prayed for me with loving encouragement during the process of writing this book. I have been blessed beyond measure and thank God for every person who cared enough to see this come to fruition.

Contents

Forward

Making Memories by the Moment

"Be hospitable to one another without complaint. As each one has received a special gift, employ it in serving one another, as good stewards of the manifold grace of God."

—1 Peter 4:9–10

Some of my earliest memories of teatime were of my mum and sister relaxing while enjoying time together with a cup of tea. My mother was born in Australia and came to the United States in her early twenties bringing English traditions into our home. I remember Mum putting the kettle on to boil in the midafternoon, pouring herself a "cuppa," and savoring something sweet. This was a time for her to sit and enjoy reading for a spell, before returning to her chores.

My sister was also born in Australia and was sixteen years my senior. She drank tea as a youngster and on into her adult years. She used her teatime to write letters during World War II, while her husband served in Germany. If she wasn't writing, she was in an easy chair enjoying a good book and sipping tea.

In spite of my English heritage, I wasn't especially fond of tea growing up. Because of this I drank it white, meaning with lots of milk and sugar. It wasn't until I became a seasoned woman that I started truly enjoying tea for the taste of it.

In England, Australia and other parts of the former British Empire, however, indulging in an afternoon cuppa is a way of life. In recent years, this quaint tradition has caught on in the United States through gathering in tearooms.

The décor of tearooms will vary; some have a charming Victorian motif and antiques, others are replicas of lovely garden settings, while still others are plain and unpretentious. Most create a similar ambiance for tea with soft music in the background. Some serve petite finger sandwiches, fruit and pastries, while others offer meat pies and quiche. All have a variety of teas with the accompanying accoutrements necessary to make the gathering possible and pleasurable.

No matter how lavish or simple the tearoom or tea event, don't forget the most important ingredient—unhurried conversation. It is a sanctuary from our fast-paced lives. Tea naturally serves as a thread that weaves memories together of happiness as well as sorrows. Make every effort to not allow time constraints to hinder the enjoyment of being together, relaxing, and sharing meaningful conversation. Remember to make room in your life and schedule for others. Share your life and find the sweetest joys mankind can know.

Achieving this goal is to practice the lost art of hospitality. I came from a poor family, and I don't remember my mother ever entertaining guests, so the idea of hosting a tea was foreign to me. However, after becoming a Christian my interest in hospitality was piqued. At a women's retreat with my church in 1979, Emarie Britten, one of the seasoned ladies, gave a seminar on hospitality. It was just what I needed to give me confidence; she made it look so easy. From that point onward I gathered as much information as possible, went to as many events as my calendar could hold, took classes, and asked a lot of questions.

Over the years Emarie has become a cherished friend, teaching and sharing with me what her mother taught her. Now I am teaching and sharing with other women. It is rewarding showing others how to give tea parties from preparation to presentation.

It has become apparent to me that many women have never put on a tea event, and may not even know where to start. For many, the desire for learning is there, but the practical knowledge is missing. While others are naturally creative, they could still benefit from helpful tips and recipes. Whether you have hosted tea gatherings or would like to, this step-by-step book written with simplicity of detail is for you.

Now I, like my mum and sister before me, often find myself relaxing with an afternoon cuppa, some tea cookies, and pleasurable reading. It is important to take that time of serenity and relish in the calm of the moment. My prayer is that you will pass this gift of hospitality on to your children or grandchildren, creating moments of blessed memories of tea gatherings or a quiet repose of your own.

Chapter One

How Did This Whole Tea Thing Start?

*I must rise at early dawn, as busy as can be, to get my
daily labor done, and pluck the leafy tea.*

—Ballad of the Tea Pickers

*B*efore we get into the planning and preparing of the tea event, let us have an introduction to tea itself and its origin. Tea is an aromatic stimulant, containing various polyphenols, essential oils and caffeine. Water is the world's most popular and least expensive beverage, but tea is second.

All of the world's tea comes from just one plant. The tea plant itself is called the Camellia sinesis. A native of Southeast Asia, this plant flourishes best in well-drained acid soil, in a warm, tropical or sub tropical climate with ample rainfall, and an altitude of at least one thousand, and no more than seven thousand feet above sea level.

Tea is brewed from the dried leaves of this plant and has been drunk in China for several thousand years. The first reliable reference to tea comes from an ancient Chinese dictionary written around 350 A.D. Tea is drunk by about half of the worlds population. Only one tea plantation exists in the United States, that being in South Carolina. It takes three to five years for the plants to become productive, and depending on the variety can have an economic life of between 40 and 100 years.

Women are generally employed as pickers because of their agility, patience, and accuracy that are uniquely "feminine" traits, essential to nurturing tea to its full charm. That sounds right to me. It takes approximately two to three thousand leaves to produce a single pound of tea. An experienced tea leaf plucker can pick enough shoots in one day to produce nine pounds of finished tea.

Tea leaves are ready to be plucked for harvest when the young shoots appear. In most regions plucking is seasonal but in the hottest climates, it is a

◈ *Sunburn:* Dampened tea cloths placed on the burned area removes the sting of the burn. Keep cloth on until the burned area begins to cool, about 15 minutes. Your skin might appear tan, but it is only from the tea and will wash off with your next bathing.

◈ *Minor cuts and abrasions:* Soak cotton balls or cotton bandage in tea solution. Apply to minor cuts or abrasions, allowing it to rest on the laceration at least five minutes. Re-apply several times a day for two days. Healing and relief should be noticed and pain reduced.

◈ *Dyeing with tea:* For dingy, faded lingerie that is still in wearable condition, dip in a tea bath. Now you have a champagne nitie. The same method can be used on a variety of fabrics. Investigate some books before taking the plunge.

You might prefer a tea solution with loose leaves, instead of tea bags. It is important not to use flavored or scented teas. Use only plain, black leaves. Store this solution in your refrigerator, ready for use.

1/2 cup black tea leaves
1 quart boiling water

Remember, strain the leaves as stated earlier, and put them in your garden, not down your garbage disposal.

Chapter Two

Making a Good Cuppa

"Come and have a cup with me."

—Inscription on a Hotel Frodsham Teapot, 1919

*H*ow to brew the perfect pot of tea seems to be a dilemma for most people. There is definitely a technique to achieve the right taste, and believe it or not it's personal preference. If it is too strong, it leaves a film on your tongue and has a bitter taste called, "tannis." This is something you definitely don't want. If it is too weak, it doesn't have any flavor, and is much like tea colored water you don't want that either. So what is the secret? Before brewing tea, there are a few simple decisions to be made. It can be any of these combinations: the brewing time, the type of tea, the difference between loose tea and tea bags.

Step 1. To begin, have all of your equipment clean and ready at your fingertips. Teakettle, teapot, cups and saucers, mesh tea strainer for loose leaves, tea, milk and sugar. Decide whether you will use tea bags or loose tea. If you are going to use a strong black tea in the bag, use one bag for each two cups. In other words, if you are using a six-cup teapot, use only three tea bags. Depending on the type of tea, you may want to add one more bag for a stronger brew. If using tea leaves, measure a full kitchen teaspoon per two cups. Again, if it is a six-cup teapot, use three full teaspoons. Anything more than that is too strong. This is something you will have to experiment with for your own taste and pleasure.

Step 2. Use freshly drawn cold water. As the water is running, notice the tiny bubbles. That means the water if full of oxygen, or aerated. Aerated water brings out the full flavor of the tea. Hot water from the tap is generally stale from standing in the water heater pipes. Bottled water is not the preference of choice either, as there is no oxygen and leaves the tea tasting flat.

Take the teakettle to the kitchen faucet and put in as much cold water as the teapot holds, whether four cups, six cups, or more. Place the kettle on the stove and bring the water to the boiling point. Once the water boils, turn off the burner and allow a few moments for it to settle; you don't want to pour bubbling hot water that could splatter and burn someone. While the water is on the stove heating, pre-heat the teapot by putting some hot water from the tap in the teapot and swirl it around. Once the water is boiled, take the teapot to the kettle, not the kettle to the teapot. In just a split second the water cools and loses oxygen, which does affect the taste of the tea.

Be sure to empty the hot water that was heating the pot, and add the proper amount of tea before adding the boiling water. If using tea bags, steep them in the teapot no more than two minutes, then remove them. They will continue steeping as long as they remain in hot water. I know most other recipes tell you to steep from three to five minutes, but I can assure you that is unfavorable to the pleasure of the tea flavor.

Try testing it for yourself. Start with two minutes and if that doesn't suit you, add another minute. A lot depends on the brand and blend of tea, so this is experiment time. Do it first for you, and maybe one or two friends, ask their opinions as well.

As mentioned earlier, smaller leaves steep quicker than larger leaves, which may take less than two minutes. Put the loose leaves in a tea filter basket. Do not use one of those cute little tea balls; it puts the tea leaves in agony. Save the tea balls to shake powdered sugar, or store potpourri. When the hot water is poured over the leaves they unfurl two to three times in size and must have room to give off their best color and flavor. The steeping time is the same as with tea bags.

Herb Tea

Did you know that herb tea is really not tea at all? It is an infusion, because the boiling water is infused with the herb, and contains no tea shrub leaves. This type of hot drink should be referred to as a tisane. Herbal concoctions are often a combination of fruit or peels, flowers, leaves, herbs or spices. At least 396 herbs and spices are available commercially for use in an herbal tisane. Because it is a milder beverage you will use one bag per cup, or one full teaspoon of loose leaves per cup. If using fresh leaves from the garden, crush the herb leaf, then steep this type of tea for three-to-five minutes to reap its full flavor. There is no caffeine with herbal tisanes, and that is a plus for those who have a reaction to caffeine and expectant mothers. All of this to say that these are simple infusions that satisfy the taste buds, and are harmless sips.

Many have planted their own herb gardens and gain the benefits of mixing the freshness of their choice of leaves. Such teas have long been used for their healing and rejuvenating qualities. Some herbs that are most common are chamomile, hyssop, ginger, ginseng, lavender, mint and basil, and there are hundreds more. It is said that chamomile tea is good for treating indigestion, insomnia, stress and anxiety. Fennel tea is the nursing mother's companion, increasing milk flow and relieving a baby's colic.

To get more information on herb tisanes, there are a number of books and web sites on herb teas and their remedies.

Tell Me More About Tea Leaves vs. Tea Bags

As you have already learned, tea comes from the Camellia sinensis plant. Leaf buds and young leaves (the tips) are used in making tea, the age of the leaves determining the taste and name of the particular commercial variety. Orange Pekoe (pronounced pek-oh, not peek-oh) is made from the youngest leaves and Souchong (sue-chong) from the fourth leaves. Formosa Oolong (oo-long) tea, grown in China, is partially fired and then steamed, thus being intermediate between green and black teas.

Since the tea known as Orange Pekoe, is most familiar with many, here is some trivia. Tomislav Podreka says, "The Chinese word Pak-ho roughly means "white or light down." The old fashioned meaning for pekoe then refers to the downy substance on the bud. Orange pekoe leaves have nothing to do with the color orange or the flavor of the citrus fruit. The term was derived from a reference to the princess of Orange. Today, orange pekoe refers to the larger of the leaves on a fine plucking and the term indicates a generally good-quality tea, and would certainly not fit in a tea bag!"

All of this to say that when the leaves are dried out in the open air they are laid individually on screens much like our window screens. At different intervals they are shaken and tossed with the residue or tea dust, filtering through the screen and then gathered for the tea bags. When tea leaves are processed, many of them break into tiny pieces called fannings. The only level of tea inferior to a fanning is dust, tea leaf dust is used for poor quality tea bags. Fanning's also find their way into tea bags and are notably better to dust in terms of flavor and aroma. As you become a connoisseur of tea taste you will definitely notice the difference between tea bags and loose tea for the best taste. The loose tea has more exquisite taste and the color seems richer, but again, it is individual choice as well as convenience. The handy little sacks usually hold inferior tea, either tea leaf dust or fannings, which results in weak, rather bland tasting tea.

Because of the versatility of the tea bag, you can take it with you wherever you go. But, once you have enjoyed the taste of the loose-leaf tea, it is sure to be your choice of tea sipping. There are three thousand varieties of tea that come from the Camellia sinensis, so you have a lot of tea tasting to do.

A New York City tea importer, Thomas Sullivan, invented the tea bag in 1908. He sent tea samples in little hand-sewn silk bags to his retail dealers and private customers. He was surprised when he received a large number of orders; the customers had found them convenient for brewing. Sullivan substituted gauze bags for silk, and the tea bag was born. In today's market, the bags are made by machine with specially treated paper fiber.

Melitta® makes a tea filter bag for brewing loose tea. I find these bags a revolutionary breakthrough for the loose tea industry. I now place my loose tea in a filter bag and can transport it wherever I choose to go, or use it at home if brewing more than one pot of tea. You can put three teaspoons in a filter bag that will accommodate a six-cup teapot. No more store bought inferior tea bags for me.

The best way to store loose-leaf tea is in opaque containers. There are so many interesting tins available that you can display on your kitchen counter, or keep them in a cool, dry place. Tea containers should have tight sealing lids. If you buy your tea in boxes with foil wrap, transfer the tea to an attractive tin. This guards against moisture and helps to preserve flavor. Like most fine foods, all tea has a shelf life of about one year. Do not put in the freezer or refrigerator.

Chapter Three

Those Dainty Little Sandwiches

*"Commit your works to the Lord, and your
plans will be established"*

—Proverbs 16:3

*T*he mainstay of a tea party that your guests can hardly wait
to try is the dainty tea sandwich. The idea is not to stuff your
guests but to satisfy them. I plan on five of the finger
sandwiches per person. Once the crusts have been
removed, this is just about right. Two slices of bread
will yield four finger sandwiches. The key is to serve
in courses and to serve from the least sweet to the most
sweet. However, some start off with scones first
(most sweet) and then the sandwiches
or, serve the scones at the same
time as the sandwiches on
the top of a tiered server.
Use a variety of breads
such as white, wheat, or
pumpernickel. Small cocktail loaves make
attractive open-faced sandwiches and you
don't have to trim these crusts. Add the fillings and cut on the diagonal and you will
have two sandwiches, cut again and you will
have four triangles. Use your imagination here. Tea
sandwiches may be closed or open faced, cut into
triangles, squares, rolled, ribbon or made
into fancy shapes (see illustrations). I do
not suggest using cookie cutters because

the bread is too thick and a lot is wasted. (Save the cutters for cookies or solid gelatin shapes.) If you do use cutters, cut the bread first then add the filling, but beware, this is tedious and very time consuming. Also you will need to plan additional sandwiches since so much bread is lost.

Suggestions for Making Tea Sandwiches

Basic Tea Sandwiches

My preference is using day old bread for tea sandwiches then freezing because it doesn't tear or crumb as the freshest bread would. For pinwheel sandwiches, you do need very fresh bread for rolling. I also buy the thin sandwich kind, one white and one of wheat. It is fun to mix these with white bread on the bottom and wheat on the top or visa versa. Some of you may live in an area that has a bakery that bakes fresh bread. Ask your bakery if they make a Pullman Loaf. If so, then order one. This loaf is custom sliced at the bakery horizontally, and yields approximately ten slices. Since the loaf is virtually larger than your standard loaf, you can get up to ten finger sandwiches from two slices. Ask your baker to tint the bread pink, blue or yellow. These are fun colors for baby showers, Easter, and Mothers' Day. Try to stay away from other colors that aren't appealing to the eye.

Get into the habit of buttering each slice of bread before adding the filling. This will help seal and prevent the bread from becoming soggy. Margarine is sometimes preferred to butter, as it does not have as distinct a flavor. Do not use diet margarine because it does not seem to seal the bread as well.

Finely textured bread, as opposed to whole grains, cuts better and gives neater edges on your sandwiches. The bread is easier to handle when you are applying the butter and filling if the crusts are still intact. Leave the crusts on the bread until your sandwiches are assembled. Spread the filling approximately 1/4 inch thick to the edges of one slice of prepared bread, and then top with second slice. Now trim the crusts and cut into desired shapes.

Of course, you will have the traditional triangle, square, and finger sandwiches. It is always visually stimulating to garnish theses sandwiches with sprigs of dill, edible flowers, and to mix the colors of bread. When making your sandwiches, keep one filling for each shape of bread. Examples of these are: triangle will be chicken walnut, the pinwheels will be egg salad with dill, cucumber will always be served on white bread cut into squares. This way you can let your guests know what they will be indulging in and maybe they will even ask for a recipe or two.

Pinwheel Sandwiches

When making pinwheels or rolled sandwiches use either fresh white or wheat bread. My preference for making pinwheels is using the Pullman loaf because when flattened with the rolling pin you get more sandwiches than with the traditional loaf. Remove the crusts and lay one slice at a time on a cutting board. Roll until flat with a rolling pin. Butter each slice and add filling leaving some space on each side. Fill sparsely and roll as tight as possible.

When you have done several rolled sandwiches, wrap tightly in plastic wrap and refrigerate until ready to slice. This can be anywhere from three to twenty-four hours. After the plastic wrap has been removed, butter the whole outside of the sandwich. Depending on the sandwich ingredients, roll it into chopped parsley, watercress, chives, or nuts. Now you can slice your chilled bread crosswise, either into two rolled sandwiches, or sliced four times which will give you the pinwheel effect. Isn't it fun to use the creativity the Lord has given to each of us for His glory and for others to enjoy?

Striped or Ribbon Sandwiches

Use one loaf of white bread, one brown loaf and perhaps a tinted color. Butter each slice on one side. Remove crusts with serrated bread knife. Build a striped effect by pressing the crust-less white and brown slices together in alternate layers with three or more fillings. Press the slices together firmly then wrap and chill. To serve, cut the bread in two-inch wide striped finger sandwiches.

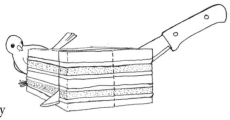

Make-Ahead Sandwiches

When entertaining a large group, I prefer to make the sandwiches the day before as there is plenty to do on the morning of the tea. Fillings made a few days in advance and refrigerated until time to assemble sandwiches helps the flavors to blend. If you follow these steps carefully, your sandwiches will not dry out and will be as fresh as when you put them together.

Use a large shallow plastic container with a lid. Or if you don't have one, the broiler pan from the oven works perfectly. Line the container with wax paper. Arrange a layer of sandwiches with crusts still intact and not yet cut into shapes. Place wax paper over the sandwiches. Continue in this manner until container is filled. Note: be sure to always have a layer of wax paper between the sandwiches. Take a tea towel that has been immersed in cold water and then wring out as dry as possible. Lay towel gently on top and drape over the sides of the pan in a wrapped manner, then refrigerate.

Remove sandwiches one at a time prior to the tea hour. On a breadboard using a sharp knife, trim crusts, cut into shapes, and then garnish. (This method of storing keeps the sandwiches nice and fresh and takes away the pressure of last minute frazzle). Arrange sandwiches on doily lined plates or trays. Cover with plastic wrap and dampened tea towels until ready to serve.

Sandwich Recipes

Following are a few of recipes that I use regularly. You will soon be able to gather various ideas from friends and other tea books, as well as experiment on your own. These should help you get off to a good start. Have fun and enjoy!

Chicken Walnut

4 boneless/skinned chicken breast halves
1/2 cup finely chopped toasted walnuts
herbed mayonnaise (see recipe)
salt to taste

Poach chicken breast halves in a small amount of salted water for 20 minutes, and then cool. Cut chicken breasts into large chunks and put into a food processor. Pulse until finely chopped. Remove chicken to bowl and add enough mayonnaise to moisten. Stir in toasted walnuts just before making sandwiches.

Stuffed Olive and Pecan Spread

8 ounces cream cheese, softened
1/2 cup mayonnaise
1/2 cup chopped pecans
1 tablespoon chopped onion
1 1/2 tablespoon butter
1/2 cup chopped stuffed green olives

Fry pecans in butter. Blend cream cheese and mayonnaise. Add olives, pecans, and onion and mix well. You will get raves on this one.

Traditional Cucumber

8 ounce cream cheese, softened
2 English hothouse cucumbers

Peel and slice cucumbers as thin as possible. Place in colander and sprinkle with salt and vinegar. Sit saucer on top to help drain for 30 minutes. Layer two to three slices on prepared bread. Sprinkle lightly with dill if desired. Cucumber sandwiches are a must at any tea party and there are a myriad of recipes and different ways you may use them; this one is simple and very English.

Lemon Cucumber

12 thin slices bread
6 tablespoons butter, softened
grated peel of one lemon
1 tablespoon lemon juice with pulp
1 small cucumber, peeled and sliced thin
fresh ground pepper
sugar

Cream butter in small bowl, add lemon peel and juice. Evenly spread each slice of bread with butter. Cover six slices of bread with thin layer of cucumber slices. Sprinkle lightly with sugar and pepper. Cover with remaining buttered bread slices. Trim crusts. Cut each sandwich into four triangles. These are a tart, refreshing change from the tried-and-true cucumber sandwiches typically served with tea. Makes 24 sandwiches.

Ritz Tea Sandwiches

The Ritz Hotel in London, serves a variety of sandwiches at their afternoon teas. One of the favorites is a combination of cottage cheese with carrots and hazelnuts.

16 slices cracked wheat bread
1/4 cup chopped toasted hazelnuts
1 cup small curd cottage cheese
fresh parsley to garnish
1/2 cup grated carrot
salt to taste

Remove crusts from bread and cut into rounds. Combine cottage cheese, carrot, and hazelnut in a medium bowl. Mix together well. Add a little salt if desired. Spread some of the mixture on top of each round. Garnish with a piece of fresh parsley. Makes 32 open-faced sandwiches.

Dilled Egg Salad

5 eggs, hard boiled and peeled
1/4 cup fresh dill, finely chopped
mayonnaise

Mash eggs, stir in fresh dill and add enough mayonnaise to reach a spreading consistence. Add enough salt and pepper to taste. To make these into pinwheel sandwiches remove crusts from white bread slices and roll with a rolling pin to flatten slightly. Spread each slice with butter and the egg salad. Roll bread jelly-roll fashion. Wrap each sandwich roll in plastic wrap tightly, twisting ends to keep out air. Refrigerate. Before serving time, remove plastic wrap and butter outside of sandwich; roll in chopped watercress or chives. Cut in half diagonally, into thirds, or several two-inch slices.

Smoky Salmon Fingers

16 ounce can red salmon, skin and bones removed; drain
8 ounces and 3 ounces cream cheese, softened
1 tablespoon finely chopped onion
2 teaspoons lemon juice
1 1/2 teaspoon prepared horseradish
1/4 teaspoon liquid smoke
1 teaspoon Worcestershire sauce

Blend all ingredients together well and refrigerate over night or until ready to make sandwiches. When you are ready to serve, and the crust has been trimmed off the bread, cut into three finger sandwiches.

Olive Tapènade

2 cups black olives, pitted
3 tablespoons capers
2 garlic cloves
6 tablespoons olive oil
2 teaspoons lemon zest, grated (carrot curls optional)

In a blender, process black olives, capers, garlic cloves, olive oil, and lemon zest until coarsely chopped. Serve open faced on cocktail rye and garnish with a carrot curl. Makes 24 sandwiches. Quite tasty.

Sandwich Spreads

A spread can be used on most anything other than an open-faced sandwich. Try them on toasted bread, sweet breads, scones, and fresh fruit. Used much like jams and jellies they are not always sweet and often times tangy.

Honey Butter

1 cup unsalted butter, room temperature
1/4 cup honey
1/4 cup powdered sugar

In a medium bowl, mix the butter, honey and sugar together until fluffy. Store in refrigerator until ready to serve.

Orange Butter

1/2 box confectioner's sugar
1/2 pound butter (2 cubes)
2 tablespoons orange juice concentrate
grated rind of two oranges

Beat sugar and butter together. Add orange juice and rind and keep soft to serve. This is great on pumpkin or date nut bread, scones, etc.

Herbed Mayonnaise

1 large egg
2 tablespoons lemon juice
2 tablespoons Dijon mustard
2 tablespoons minced fresh chives
2 tablespoons capers
1 small clove garlic
1/4 teaspoon salt
1 cup olive oil

In blender, combine egg, lemon juice, mustard, chives, capers, garlic, and salt. With motor running, slowly pour in oil in a thin, steady stream. Process 30 seconds or until thickened. Cover and chill.

Fresh Herb Spread

8 ounces cream cheese, softened
1 tablespoon fresh lemon juice
Tabasco to taste
1/2 cup fresh herbs of choice
paprika

Mix cream cheese, lemon juice and Tabasco well and combine with 1/2 cup of fresh herbs. Spread on buttered bread and sprinkle with paprika.

Artichoke Spread

6 ounce jar marinated artichoke hearts
1/2 teaspoon salt
6 ounces cream cheese, softened
5 tablespoon sour cream
1/4 teaspoon garlic salt
1 tablespoon white wine

Drain artichokes and chop fine. Add to remaining ingredients, blending well.

Strawberry Cream Cheese

Blend one 8-ounce package of softened cream cheese with 1/4 cup strawberry preserves. Stir in 3 tablespoons chopped pecans. Spread on date nut bread and garnish with pecan halves.

Assorted Tea Sandwich Suggestions:

- Smoked turkey with raspberry mayonnaise on cracked wheat bread.
- Shrimp with dill vinaigrette on oatmeal bread.
- Ham with thin pineapple slices on dill bread.
- Asparagus spears with lemon mayonnaise on wheat bread, or rolled in sliced ham.
- Egg and tomato—add sharp grated cheese on pumpernickel bread
- Avocado with sprouts and walnuts on whole wheat bread.

Trivia: The idea of afternoon tea began around the 1700s as a way to ward off hunger pangs before dinner. This tradition led the Earl of Sandwich to make his famous invention—the sandwich—by putting meats or other fillings between two pieces of bread.

Chapter Four

Setting the Tea Table

"They sat down to tea—the same party round the same table."

—Jane Austen, *Emma*

The presentation of the tea table is of utmost importance and sets the stage for the whole tea celebration. If you don't already have some lovely white, pastel or floral linens, start making a collection of them. Watch for the white sales at department stores. Go to garage sales, thrift stores, and sift through the linens at antique shops.

Soft, floral prints are nice and fresh for an outdoor garden tea. Try to purchase tablecloths of a polyester blend, as they are easiest to care for. A lace topper of some kind does enhance the Victorian look, but is not necessary. Depending on the theme, it might be something nice to have on hand.

Please, no paper napkins (serviettes). Serviette is a French word for napkin and used extensively in British speaking countries. I like to use that word at teatime to keep with the English tradition. Though there are a myriad of lovely paper designs and qualities to choose from, your tea party loses the charm of elegance when paper is used. This is one time you want to use your best for those you care about. As long as the setting is gracious and elegant, the tea party can take place anywhere you wish.

Flowers are an absolute must on your tea table; they bring in God's creativity and color from outdoors, as well as softening the moment. You can either have a centerpiece (not so high that people can't see the others across the table) or individual bouquets in small vases at each place setting. It makes your guests feel pampered to have their own flowers to pick up and inhale the fragrance, if they so desire. Sprinkle rose petals randomly on the table. Rose petals are abundant during the late spring and summer months in many areas, as are pansy faces in the winter. Use these same petals on your sandwiches, fruit, or dessert plates as a finishing touch to tie things together. Some flowers are edible, with different and interesting flavors and should be washed and pesticide free. Try some; it's fun to indulge in new things that aren't sinful.

Tea Tip: To have rose petals and pansies available to sprinkle on the tea table at any time of the year, here is a clever way to preserve them. When the flower of your choice is at it's peak, cut it from the plant, carefully remove the petals and place them one by one between the pages of your telephone directory. Let them stay for about ten days to pull all of the moisture from the petal. When they are dry, place them in layers in a clear plastic box with wax paper in between. The petals are not crispy dry so that they break easily, but are soft and almost silk-like to the touch and can be used over and over. The next time you are giving a tea party you will have all of the petals you need for the finishing touch and your guests will marvel. As we cover the different types of tea celebrations, I will give you exact details of what should be on the tea table for each event.

"Thou dost prepare a table before me" (Psalm 23:5).
God is our abundant provider!

Cream Tea

What, in your opinion, is a cream tea? Vast majorities of people think that a cream tea is tea served with a variety of cream puffs, éclairs, or desserts filled with whipped cream. Some think it just means using cream in their tea. However, a cream tea is tea served with a scone (the English pronounce it "scawn" as in "lawn") accompanied with jam and Devonshire cream.

Note: I will be referring to Devonshire cream or Devon cream throughout the table settings. This cream comes from Devonshire, England, where the cows are fed and bred much differently than in America. The grazing lands are very lush with fertile soil, producing rich creamy milk. As the milk settles, the thick cream rises to the top, is scraped off and used for delicate pastries. The cream is not pasteurized. Clotted cream and Devonshire cream are very similar and can be found in specialty import shops. A mock recipe for this will be found in the recipe section of this book.

Cream tea is probably the most conventional type of tea you will serve, and it is by far the most popular in England. Small teashops all over England have signs hanging outside announcing "cream tea." You are served an open-faced scone with a dab of jam on one side and a dab of cream on the other plus

a pot of tea. Sugar and a milk jug are also on the table as well as a spoon for stirring. Nothing more. It's the warmth of the amber liquid and friendship that are most important to the tea affair. This is the best time to serve flavored teas. There is such a variety to choose from and interesting infusions to test the palate.

> *"Come, oh come, ye tea-thirsty restless ones;*
> *the kettle boils, bubbles and sings musically."*
>
> —Rabindranath Tagor

The setting of the table for a cream tea is rather simple, and doesn't require a variety of implements. Always start with a fresh tea cloth. If this is an item that you are short on, as mentioned earlier you can start collecting them from antique shops, garage sales, grandma's attic or wherever. Lovely linens are available in a variety of sizes, textures and colors. When a friend drops in for tea and if you will be sitting at a table, spread a tea cloth first. Again it makes one feel special and sets the tone for an enjoyable time.

While the kettle is getting ready to boil, on a serving tray place the teacups and saucers with a four-inch paper doily between them, an eight-inch or nine-inch tea plate, spoons, tea knife to spread the jam, serviettes, milk, sugar, scones, Devon cream, jam and lemon curd, if desired. Include a flower from the garden if possible, or a lovely artificial arrangement; candles are a nice touch and add softness. By now the kettle has boiled and you have added tea to the pot and everything is ready. Carry the serving tray to your tea table and arrange all of these items on the table that you adorned with the tea cloth, now enjoy the sweet fellowship.

Tea Tip: Make your scones from scratch, double the recipe and drop by the spoonful on a wax paper baking sheet, and then freeze. When frozen, remove from the baking sheet and place into a zip-lock bag by the dozen, then back to the freezer. They will be ready for company anytime someone unexpected drops in. Just add two minutes to the baking time for frozen scones. See recipe section for ingredients and baking time.

Afternoon Tea

*"There are few hours in life more agreeable
than the hour dedicated to the ceremony
known as afternoon tea."*

—Henry James

As the name suggests, afternoon is the time this tea is served and probably is the most highly noted for the "tea party." The wonderful thing about the afternoon tea party is the variations to which you can serve and decorate. It can be lavish and formal, or simple and casual; it will depend on the occasion, and the tone of the invitations. The most fun is the planning of both the menu, and the decorating. Since we live in America, our afternoon time is usually from noon to about three o'clock. In England it is more like four o'clock. Our eating habits are much different than theirs, so the timing of our events will differ from their tradition. More than just a cuppa, afternoon tea is an elegant snack and the bonding of friends.

Buffet Tea

*"The tea table was set under the trees. It was
a lovely sight…There were pyramids of
strawberries and raspberries…and cakes
with sugared icing."*

—Consuela, Duchess of Marlbourough

For most people the word buffet connotes a party atmosphere. Buffet teas are wonderful for large groups, bridal or baby showers, graduations, queen for a day, or birthday parties. Be creative. People love to dress up and be together. When you are having more than 12 guests, as mentioned before, it is advisable to have help. Ask some of your best friends with whom you work well. It makes the load much lighter, and you can share in the fun together.

Since each of us has a different amount of room in which to set up a tea of this size, I will suggest a general setting and you can elaborate as much as you wish to adjust to your surroundings. Visualize a long table, perhaps your dining table with leaves added or an eight-foot buffet pushed against a wall and covered with a white linen cloth and topped with lace. Pulled up at each corner will be

a table-tussie made from either fresh or artificial flowers and flowing ribbons in your theme color.

You will want your buffet table to be as beautiful as possible, so have an exquisite floral centerpiece and gleaming silver pieces. Candles are always nice, even during the afternoon, but not necessary. Candlelight seems to have a softening effect and gives a romantic touch. Having different heights of serving pieces makes for an interesting table.

If you don't have a cake plate on a pedestal, turn one of your sturdy goblets upside down and place a plate on top to give you the same effect, or a cup upside down with it's saucer on top.

For illustration purposes let us suppose this is an afternoon celebration (this will determine the food that will be served). Moving from left to right, your guest picks up a plate and moves along the table choosing different flavored sandwiches, scones, fruit, stuffed cherry tomatoes or chicken tarts (see illustration on previous page).

At a tea table a pourer is waiting to serve. The server chooses a cup and saucer and asks, "Would you like your tea plain or with milk, sugar, honey, or lemon?" When the tea is prepared, the guest goes to an assigned table that is waiting for her pleasure and is seated.

The tables will already have been set with the needed flatware along with a serviette, water jug and glass, jam, lemon curd and Devon cream (for the scones) a small floral piece or tea candles in votive cups. When your guest is in need of a tea refill she goes back to the tea table and is served.

If this should be a stand-up affair with limited seating, put just one or two sandwiches on your tea plate, then go around the room and visit. You can always go back for more food.

If you are sitting in a chair or on a sofa with a table within reach, rest your cup and saucer on the table. When you want to have a taste of tea, bring both the cup and saucer to waist level, raise the cup to your lips and take a sip. Think of the cup and saucer as one unit, the saucer should not be more than twelve inches between you and the table your beverage is resting on. In other words, don't leave the saucer on the table and bring the single cup to your mouth. If anything should be spilled, it will go into the saucer and not your lap or their carpet.

Another choice for a large gathering is to have separate tables for your guests. Let's say four tables with eight guests each. Appoint a hostess at each table to keep the teapot full and replenish the food. The guest tables would already be set with tea plates, serviettes, flatware, milk and sugar, jam, lemon curd, Devon cream and of course the food on tiered servers. It is also a nice time to use place cards, and party favors if you are giving them. Since there will be 40 sandwiches in unique shapes and with various fillings at each table, you would use each tier of your plate server. Name cards of the different sandwiches are a nice complement, and then no one has to guess. There may be separate plates for the scones. Don't forget the flowers.

Like most of us, you probably don't have 32 teacups in your possession. Ask each person to bring her favorite teacup and saucer. Your guest will find her place and then put her own teacup and saucer on the table. As the tea is being poured, ask each lady at her own table to share about how her teacup is special, where it came from, who might have given it to her as a gift, or if it is an heirloom from a relative. This is an icebreaker, and it's fun to hear the many stories told.

So far dessert hasn't been mentioned, saving the best for last. Serving desserts buffet style is the easiest for a grand assortment of enticements. Don't stop at anything. Be sure to have sponge cake, lemon tarts, cream puffs sprinkled with chocolate and powdered sugar, cookies, date nut bread, sugared grapes, chocolate dipped strawberries and of course at least two different types of English trifle. Use some of your favorite specialty recipes.

This is the perfect time to randomly scatter your table with dried or fresh rose petals, even pansy faces as suggested for effect earlier in this chapter.

Chapter Five

Planning a Tea Event for 100 to 500 Ladies

Whatever you do, do your work heartily, as for the
Lord rather than for men.

—Colossians 3:23

When considering a large group it takes considerable thought and organization for your tea event to be successful. Many willing and helping hands will be necessary. The first things are:

- ❧ Pray
- ❧ Plan
- ❧ Prepare

A tea celebration is a big undertaking and very detailed, which requires plenty of time to plan, and the cooperation of many. When working with the body of Christ, projects like this seem to flow with much ease. Above all else, keep this project in constant prayer. Ask for the Lord's guidance, and for just the right ladies to help make this gathering a success.

You, the reader, will possibly be the coordinator of this occasion. You will have the most information for it to be a success. Depending on how your organization or ministry functions, there will be different levels of accountability for those working with you. For the type of tea I'm describing, an individual table hostess will be responsible for the table settings. Decide why you are having this tea celebration. Is it for Mother's Day, a church celebration, a fundraiser or a women's outreach? A chairperson will need to be selected for each of the following:

- ❧ Theme and Speaker
- ❧ Publicity
- ❧ Cost and Budget
- ❧ Program and Tickets

- ✿ Ticket Sales
- ✿ Room Set Up
- ✿ Table Hostess
- ✿ Escorts and Waiters
- ✿ Table Favors/Donation of Gifts
- ✿ Food Service/Beverage
- ✿ Order of Event
- ✿ Clean Up

The first thing on the agenda is to choose a date and location. Once you have reserved the facility, you will want to select your chairpersons and have a planning meeting. After the initial meeting, try to come together on a monthly basis, or more often if necessary to stay on top of things.

The goal is for things to run smoothly and to honor the Lord. With this many willing servants working together, it is best to keep the communication line open.

After the chairpersons have been assigned their tasks, they should then select a committee for additional help. Be sure they understand what is expected of them. Give each one a written outline to refer to, including your name and phone number at the top so they can contact you if necessary.

Theme and Speaker

Select an event chairperson who will take charge of the entire program. The coordinator can't do it all. After the theme has been chosen, there should be some plan of action. The event chairperson should contact a speaker that is suggested by the coordinator. The speaker should be able to speak on the theme chosen, and be able to cover it well. Thirty to forty minutes is ample time to allow for a speaker. Along with the speaker, have music as part of the program, such as two or three solos with appropriate lyrics that are honoring to the Lord. If at all possible, have a piano or CD's playing in the background while the ladies are partaking of their wonderful edibles.

Publicity

It is wise to place an ad in your church bulletin and local newspaper. Advertise the upcoming event, time, place and cost. Have flyers printed to place in various businesses. Do this at least three to four months in advance, and have regular reminders of the upcoming tea. When it is time for ticket purchases, give a deadline of about three weeks before the tea.

The publicity chairperson will assign someone to have programs designed and printed with an outline of the program. The tickets should correspond to the theme.

Cost and Budget

Before you can give an estimated cost for tickets, the budget will have to be set. This is a bit challenging, because some of the things can't be bought until closer to the affair. The chairperson will have to do some legwork and investigating to come as close as possible to a total amount for goods purchased.

First, make a list of everything you will need, and itemize it accordingly. Find out the cost of renting linens, centerpieces, and publicity, printing costs such as flyers, tickets and programs. There are sometimes hidden costs that you may not think of, such as flowers or plants for the ladies bathrooms. Are there going to be flowers or any other decorations for the platform? The larger costs are obvious, like the speaker's fee, printing for publicity, table numbers and hostess' name for each table, program and tickets, food and beverage, linens, charge for using a rented facility if you are using one, and whatever else you decide on. Be realistic, and maybe sometimes a bit high in pricing so that you don't go in the red.

To figure what to charge for the tickets, use the following as an example to plan for 300 ladies. Based on eight people per table, add your total figure for linens and centerpieces and divide by eight. Then take the fee for a rental facility, all printing, speaker fee (honorarium, gift, and transportation costs if there are any), gifts for guests, and additional floral arrangements. Are you paying the Mistress of Ceremonies, vocalist, pianist and publicity? Include every expense you can think of. Now that you have a figure, divide your total cost by 300 so each guest is helping with overall expenses. Add the individual charge for the linens/centerpieces to the amount for the other costs to get the overall cost of the tickets.

Sometimes there may be additional expenses you might not think of, allow a little extra for these. For example, if you have estimated $14.40 for expenses per ticket, round it off to $15 per ticket.

If this amount is too high for your group, look for places to cut costs. Perhaps a florist or nursery will give you a special rate on flowers or plants. If you set your budget for $3,600, then you can charge $12 per ticket and come out on top. There might be a few dollars left over for something special such as personal table favors, or a larger gift to the speaker.

Programs and Tickets

Long before the budget has been set, the programs should have been thought out and the artwork done. The program might include some of the following information:

- ❧ On the inside left cover could be the detailed menu
- ❧ The right side of the program in order of succession:

    Table tour

    Welcome of guests and musical prelude

    Tea time blessing

    Vocal or instrumental solo

    Tea is served

    Special guest of honor will be introduced, giving her name, some background as well as the topic on which she is going to speak

    Acknowledgements and closing comments

    One last solo

    Benediction

- ❧ On the outside back cover or an added page, you could also include a list of tables, their theme and their hostess' name plus table number. It will depend on how much information you want to put on the program.

In addition, it is nice to include a special "thank you" to the many servants that helped make the whole event happen. They enjoy seeing their name in print, and it is a nice way to acknowledge their servant hearts.

Make a mock-up sample of what you want the program to look like before taking it to a printer. The tickets should have the same artwork and theme as the program. Also included should be the date, time, location, and cost. Contact a printer well in advance so that there will be plenty of time to produce your pieces.

Ticket Sales

When tickets go on sale approximately six weeks before the tea, collect all the money. If you don't, you may find yourself spending a lot of time calling people to obtain balances, then having to make arrangements as to how you are going to get payment. As you hand the lady her paid ticket put a number on it that will coincide with a table number. As the tickets are sold, it will be necessary to keep track of the seating for each table so that only eight tickets are sold for each. It might be helpful to number the tickets ahead of time with a table number and also one through eight for the ladies who will be sitting at that table, so that you can easily tell how many tickets remain for each table. Remember the table hostess will be one of the eight, so in reality you are selling to seven guests.

Have a leeway of approximately 15 extra people. Some that planned on coming might not be able to, and some who didn't buy tickets in time will suddenly find they have the chance to attend.

Refunds should be honored up to three weeks before the tea. It is wise to include a statement about this in the publicity. It can eliminate hurt feelings for those who cancel later. Any time after the deadline, money will already be going into supplies, as well as food, decorations and other things. When the day of the event arrives, have a table outside of the tearoom where you will be collecting the tickets, tearing off the stubs with the numbers going back to the guest and sending them to their escorts (to be explained later).

Room Set Up

The chairperson that will be in charge of the room set up will need to contact someone in the custodial department of your church, or the contact person of a rented facility. I prefer not to have more than nine chairs to a 60" round table; eight is better for comfort and ease. Calculated on 300 guests, with eight ladies per table, you will need 24/60"round tables with 300 chairs. You can always add a chair later if additional people arrive.

Order from the linen company 24 round tablecloths, or 85" x 85" square in the theme color chosen for the event. A few extra cloths are a good idea if you want to have any kind of a draping effect, or some should arrive soiled. I prefer the square tablecloths because they hang long enough that they fit the round tables perfectly.

Usually the round tablecloths are more costly to rent and sometimes skimpy. If you should have drink stations, book or merchandise tables, consider ordering buffet size clothes for these. Order 300 napkins of either the same color or a contrasting color depending on the look you are trying to achieve. It is suggested that you order at least 25 extra napkins. Some are at times in poor condition, and it is also good to have extras for unexpected guests. This chairperson will also be responsible for getting the tables dressed and napkins folded in plenty of time for the table settings to be arranged. It would be wise to have two or three helpers start at least the day before.

Table Hostess

Assign one lady to each individual table to be a hostess for that table. The hostess would be responsible for the china, flatware, and table decorations. She can take complete charge of the setting, or delegate it to someone else.

When creating the centerpiece, keep in mind the height. You do not want to obstruct the view of your neighbor across the way. The china does not have to be of the same design. In fact, odd matching patterns add charm to the uniqueness of each table, and are a topic of conversation.

Since only finger food will be served, your table will be set with an 8" or 9" tea plate, in other words, a salad plate. Because this is a tea, it becomes a tea plate. It is very eye appealing when placing your cups and saucers on the table to put a 4" paper doily between them. Add a butter knife (for the scones), and spoons for stirring the tea. Place two sets of milk and sugar servers on each table to avoid reaching. Do not use cream; because of the acid in the tea, cream often curdles. Any kind of regular milk works fine. Sugar cubes are my preference because they aren't as messy as granulated sugar, and ladies love to say, "two lumps please." If you choose to use cubes, be sure to supply sugar tongs. If you use granulated sugar, separate spoons for each lady are appropriate. Have small spoons for the whipped cream and jam; for these, you will need two sets of small glass containers for each table.

Another responsibility for the table hostess is to make each of her guests feel cared for and welcome. There may be one lady that would benefit from an encouraging word or gentle touch. We never know what circumstances a guest might have dealt with recently, and she may need additional attention.

Greet each lady and be sure she is introduced to everyone else at the table. Have a couple of icebreaker questions to ask that will involve each to participate. Here are some suggestions:

□ Who had freckles as a youngster?

□ Who was born outside the U.S.?

□ Who cannot swim?

The hostess should include everyone at the table in conversation, and not talk only to her friends. A tea I attended recently was delightful in every aspect except the table situation. The centerpiece was a collection of lovely dolls that were placed on different levels, making it much too high as well as wide. I never did see the ladies on the other side of the table, and spoke very little to the lady on my right, since she was involved with her friend. My friend was on my left, so we conversed the most. This was not my choice, because this could have been a time of sweet treasured memories and making new acquaintances.

When the event has finished, the table hostess will be responsible to remove everything that she brought to set the table. The only things that will be left will be the linens. The clean up committee will take care of the tablecloth and napkins.

Escorts and Waiters

Would you believe that the men you know really do enjoy serving and making your time more enjoyable? Some choices could be husbands, sons, relatives, boyfriends, and college or seminary students. One waiter can serve two tables without any trouble. Since you know how many tables there are, you will need half that amount of men. As mentioned before, these same men can be escorts.

As stated earlier, when the guests arrive have a man at the door ready to escort the ladies to their table. It might be wise to ask how many are in the group, so they can be taken all at once. It is a wonderful experience to be greeted at the door and be escorted to your table. Don't think for a minute that the men don't enjoy this, they do. In fact, they will usually ask to be put on the call list for next year. Some of you may not particularly want men being involved in the tea celebration; this is only a suggestion and makes a more relaxing time for the table hostesses.

The duty of the waiters will be to pour the tea, serve the sandwiches, scones, whipping cream and jam. They should be aware of replenishing the milk, sugar, whip cream and jam when necessary, and of course, keeping the teacups filled. When this portion of the meal is finished, then the desserts can be served. If a guest should ask for water, refer her to the nearest drinking fountain. Water isn't the main beverage at this luncheon, and the guest won't mind. When the plates are empty, the waiter should ask if the person is finished, then remove the plate.

Waiters should serve on the right side of the guest and remove plates from the left. The teacups can be lifted for refill, but must have the saucer with it. Pour away from the person so as not to accidentally spill hot liquid on her.

Table Favors

Pray for the Lord to lead you to the right local merchants to ask if they would be willing to donate 300 gifts for your ladies who are attending your event. You will be amazed how accommodating they will be, especially if they know this is a church function. Be sure to thank them for their generosity and kindness, first with a thank you note, then the next time you do business with them. This will be appreciated. Their name could even be printed on the program for an easy reminder.

If you know a group of women who enjoy crafts, get them together several months in advance to start making something appropriate for a keepsake. Some ideas are crocheted crosses, a lace bag filled with potpourri, or maybe a candle. See Chapter Eight for more favor ideas. Use your creative talents. The ladies that attend are so appreciative of any thoughtfulness, and will remember the kindness shown them for months to come.

Food Service

The food supervisor will choose the menu. This is not the time to have too much variety. Scones are a standard tea item. Ask two or three ladies to make 100 each, depending on how many people you are expecting. Scones are best if made fresh the day of the event. If prepared in dough form and frozen (uncooked), they can be baked that morning and served at room temperature. Two or three months prior to the tea is as long as scones should be kept frozen. This is a very effective way to make a large quantity of baked goods. Serve with whipped cream and raspberry or strawberry preserves (see recipe section of this book).

Making a large amount of tea is often a dilemma, but it doesn't have to be. Most churches or rented facilities have large coffee urns. Use the urns after they have been cleaned thoroughly, and had a vinegar bath to eliminate the coffee taste.

As a rule, I use tea bags for this project, and only make one flavor of tea. This is not a time for choices. Purchase any well-known tea, such as Morning Breakfast, PG Tips, Typhoo or Earl Grey. Again, we are using the number of

300 for estimates. We are estimating three cups of tea per guest, which is approximately what most people will drink. You can adjust to whatever number of persons you might have. If you are going to be making 900 cups of tea, buy 450 tea bags. Fill the urn with cold water from the tap to however many cups it holds. Put in the center post and basket. Let's say it is a 50-cup urn. Place 23 to 25 tea bags in the basket to perk. Each urn takes approximately a half hour to perk. Leave the tea bags in the basket until it is time for another batch of tea to be made. The tea won't get any stronger because the bags aren't sitting in hot water. You might want to make an extra 100 cups for the real tea lover. It would be a considerate thing to have an herbal tea available for any pregnant woman, or those that may have caffeine intolerance. I wouldn't offer it, but if asked for you would have it.

> *When you're up to your neck in hot water, be*
> *like a teapot and start to sing*

With this magnitude of people, four or five-finger sandwiches per person should suffice. Each sandwich should have a different filling. Have at least four desserts to follow. Don't forget your servants will want to eat, too. Perhaps you would like an addition of fruit, filled cherry tomatoes, carrot curls and possibly edible flowers. They look lovely spread among the plates, and people enjoy them.

If sandwiches seem too much to conquer at this time, then serve fruit and desserts. Some thoughts might be lemon bars, cream puffs, date nut bread (these should be cut into finger slices), pecan tassies, small bunches of grapes or fresh strawberries. Assign someone to provide the desserts. There are many small finger desserts in the frozen section of your discount warehouses or your local market.

Some things are easy to bake and slice individually, such as date nut bread, or small tarts. If someone is only doing this for one table, it isn't too overwhelming. Stick to the same recipe throughout the tables.

Order of Event

It is helpful to label each table with a number, the title of the table theme as well as the name of the gracious hostess. Upon arrival have an escort meet the ladies at the door and walk them to their table. As the tickets are sold; a number was put on each ticket that will match the table number. This will enable the escort to guide the lady to the appropriate table. After the guests know where they are sitting, they will want to walk around and enjoy all the varied table settings. Do allow time for this. The ladies may get inspired to give a tea of their own, or get involved in helping you next year.

To get things underway, have your Mistress of Ceremonies ask the ladies to find their seats so the tea can begin. Have a musical prelude of classical selections while the ladies are finding their way to their tables. When all are seated, welcome them and say a blessing before they partake of the food. You might want a solo at this point, and then the guests can start their luncheon. Allow approximately 30 to 45 minutes for the meal to be finished.

To make closure to mealtime have another solo, and then introduce the Guest of Honor. Be sure to give her name and some of her background as well as the topic on which she is going to speak. When the speaker is finished, give acknowledgements and closing comments. Have another solo if time allows, and then the benediction. Be sure to thank your guests for attending, and tell them that you hope that their time was uplifting and will be memorable.

Clean Up

Yes, this has to be done too. Please don't start to clean up until everyone has been dismissed and the room has cleared of guests. We don't want to seem eager for the event to be over, and maybe someone might need to linger and talk.

Each chairperson at this point should know what part they play in the cleaning up and taking down. It should be done quietly and efficiently. The area that has been used should be left in an orderly manner and in good condition, if not better than it was found. We are being witnesses for the Lord Jesus Christ, especially if this is a rented facility. It is important to leave a good image to honor Him. Give an overall look to the rest of the room to see if there is anything left undone or left behind.

Then there is the kitchen area. Wash any and all dishes, clean out coffee and tea urns thoroughly, put everything back in its original place, and wash the floors. Leave it sparkling and shiny. You may want to use this facility again. It isn't only what you do that is important, but how you do it.

Chapter Six

How to Have a Successful Children's Tea Party

"Children are the hands by which we take hold of heaven."

—Henry Ward Beecher

*I*f you are fortunate enough to have children in your life, you are truly blessed. For a long period of time my grandchildren lived several hundred miles away, which was difficult for me. I made a point of getting to know young families in the church and began to spiritually adopt their children as grandchildren. The sound of their darling little voices calling "Nanny" and running across the church campus with their arms wide open to give a hug to me made my heart always leap with joy. What a welcoming gift of love! They had no idea what it meant for this seasoned woman.

There is no reason to be lonely for children, they are everywhere, just go out and find them; you will have a refreshed look on life. If you don't have children of your own, I am sure your friends or neighbors do. The parents would be grateful for a break if you would be so inclined to take the wee one for a few hours, for both your enjoyment and the child's. Be a surrogate grandmother to a child who doesn't have the privilege of a grandmother close by, or one at all. My little adopted grandchildren are ages nine to about twelve now, and it is getting awkward for the older boys to hug as freely as they used to, so I always ask. They are becoming young adults.

Two years ago my daughter and family moved fairly close to me. It has been too wonderful for words to have my precious granddaughters near by. We are building memories of scrapbooks about life for them to reminisce over in years to come. We do all kinds of fun things together; planning their birthday party is the most exciting of all.

One of the more popular birthday parties in recent years has been a tea party for little girls who will soon become young ladies. It can be given in your own home or garden, a park, or if it is in your budget you can perhaps go to a facility that just caters to children.

A good rule of thumb: don't over invite. With too many children it becomes chaotic and confusing. Have as many children as the child is old, unless the group is mature enough to handle a few more. At my granddaughter Alec's tea party, there were eight girls for her fifth birthday. Most of the girls were between five and six years old and I knew they had good behavioral training.

The Invitation

Whatever you do, do it with kindness and love.

—The book of 1st Corinthians

For this particular birthday, I chose a teddy bear theme. When you select a theme, use it to the fullest in everything. Most stationary and variety stores carry a wide selection of children's birthday invitations with matching paper goods. I prefer to make my own at home from supplies on hand. This is a good learning experience for the child in how to be thrifty and creative.

Trace the outline of a bear on brown construction paper using a cookie cutter. Fold the paper and cut out the form leaving the fold in tact. On the inside write to whom it's for, where it is going to be, the time the party starts and ends, and ask each child to bring their favorite teddy bear. On the outside you can decorate it any way you feel. I chose to put a pink ribbon in the ear, and made the eyes, nose, and mouth with a felt marker.

When the little girls arrived in their pretty party dresses and their friendly bear under their arms, they were given a cinnamon bear necklace with their name on the back and the date of the event to wear and have as a keepsake.

For the pattern, use a miniature bear cookie cutter for the shape and put a hole in the top with either an ice pick or an awl and thread a $1/8"$ ribbon through the hole for the hanger. Be creative and imaginative. It is so much fun to see what you can come up with (see the cinnamon bear recipe at the end of this chapter.)

The Tea Table

An old wooden wagon was the table centerpiece, with several sizes and shapes of bears and a cloth book all about bears, from which a short story was read. There was a paper place mat for each guest with the same bear design as her invitation. They were placed at the table for the children to color.

The tea table was set with child size tea sets, and each girl had her own china teacup and saucer, as well as a small plate for their tea sandwiches. They were able to pour their beverage from child size teapots. Some preferred to drink apple juice, which is fine. (As long as they are drinking it from teacup, it is considered tea.)

To the right of the cookie plate was a serviette (napkin), which was an antique handkerchief. Start collecting them because they are charming, and have sweet sentiments. Ask granny; you'd be surprised what she has up her sleeve. Hankies are just the right size for little hands. It was explained how to use them. "Blot the corners of your mouth, not mop your face or use the sleeves of your garment." This is a perfect time to teach them social graces if they haven't already learned them. Refreshing the memory never hurts either. As for posture, sit straight at the table (no elbows please) with the serviette in the lap. If you are using a spoon to stir, don't tinkle the side of the cup. Stir in a little circle in the center of the cup, and then replace your spoon on the saucer. Pick up the cup and sip from it (not slurp) then gently return it to the tea saucer. And of course, "Please pass the jam," "Thank you," or "May I please have another cup of tea?" Cross legs at the ankles, not at the knees or keep the feet flat on the floor. It is never too soon to teach little girls how to become young ladies with good table manners and etiquette. Here is a little ditty that I learned as I was growing up; "Three little words I use with ease, pardon me, thank you, and if you please." This is cute and catchy to remember.

Menu

As in any entertaining event, pray, plan and prepare. Have all of your food purchased at least three days before and make anything you can as far in advance as possible so that you won't be harried when the party time starts.

For this particular birthday I chose food that I thought most children would eat. Deviled egg, peanut butter and jelly, sliced turkey with cheese, colored round cereal, and gelatin shapes. For the egg sandwiches, bread was pre-cut into heart shapes and spread first with butter then the egg mixture. Always butter bread before any other ingredient is put on it. This will keep the bread from tearing and getting soggy. For the peanut butter and jelly, I used both white and wheat bread. Butter bread first, spread peanut butter on the white side and the jelly on the brown side. Remove crusts with sharp serrated knife and cut into quarters. Stack two sandwiches with brown and white sides together and tie with either curling ribbon or 1/8" satin ribbon. The kids didn't even notice the cute little packages, but I had a good time doing it. Tell the children, when they untie their sandwich, "Think of it as a gift from Jesus, He is the bread of life."

For the turkey and cheese, also use both white and wheat bread, remove crusts and cut into strip like finger sandwiches.

Fill nut cups with colored round cereal for nibble food and gelatin cut in shapes of teddy bears using the same cookie cutter used on the invitation. Now for dessert: a tan colored coconut furry bear cake served with both vanilla and chocolate of ice cream.

The beverage for this tea was "Fairy Tea," which is a powdered strawberry mix blended with milk. Don't tell them what "Fairy Tea" is—it goes along with the mystique of the tea party. What fun they all had, especially with child size china. "This is the best tea party ever," said one little girl.

Game Time

For the familiar game of Duck, Duck, Goose, we played Teddy Bear, Teddy Bear, Cubby Bear. They each had a wonderful time running around the circle with their treasured friend. Each girl shared the name of their bear, why they named them that, and the reason it was so special to them. Theme parties are fun and should be carried out as much as possible. We also played the old favorite of musical chairs and blazing bear, which is really hot potato.

Craft Ideas

Have the children make musical instruments and sing songs. To make a tambourine take two-paper plates, have the children color and decorate them, put a few beans between the two and staple shut.

Make rain sticks with paper towel rolls or two toilet paper rolls. Glue wrapping paper or construction paper around towel rolls, cover one end with aluminum foil, put some rice and beans inside, then cover the other end with foil. Tape the foil so it doesn't slip off. Now you're ready for some songs like "Polly Put the Kettle On," "I'm A Little Tea Pot" or "Tea For Two." This will bring out the little girl in you too and give you a merry heart. Children have many interests; listen to them and take advantage of what their new thing is and make that your theme. It is wonderful to be inventive. Give a little love to a child and you get heaps back.

Children are a gift from the Lord.

—The Book of Psalms

To end the day, a photograph of the birthday child and each guest with their teddy friend was taken with a Polaroid camera and sent home as a souvenir. Take a lot of photos as you can never recapture this time. You are making a memory the children will have for many years

Tea Attire

For a little girl's tea, you can also have a dress-up party. That means you gather all of the supplies: hats, dresses, jewelry, gloves, shoes, and don't forget the makeup. You can request they come dressed, but it is always more fun to do it together. They love getting dressed in fancy clothes and acting like grown women. Just watch how they change once they are dressed and hair done differently and some makeup on. They are no different than we are, just smaller in frame. Listen to all of the giggles and laughter. They delight in acting like grown ups. Start collecting fancy formal things from thrift stores for only pennies. You can find gloves at garage sales, or maybe ask grandma, you never know what she may have stored in her attic.

Keep this type of party rather small, no more than six to eight guests unless you have help for the makeup application. It is always wise to have an extra pair of hands to keep things flowing. There are a few children's tea rooms in the area where I live that cater to dress-up parties that charge an enormous price for this kind of pampering.

If you don't already have hats, let the children make them from paper plates. Cut out the center of the plate, have bits and pieces of feathers, fabric, lace, beads, etc. Ask some of your friends if they have anything like this they don't want anymore. They are more than willing to get rid of their cast-offs, which will become your treasure. Let the girls glue till their hearts are content with an "anything goes" attitude. They do come up with some interesting creations and they are proud of them. Put ribbon ties on the hat and make a big bow under the chin. These can go home with them to play dress-up at another time.

My other granddaughter recently turned five. This is a good age to start them with a tea party. Jordyn loves being a girl. She puts on dress-up clothes whenever she can and pretends to be a princess. Because of her interest, I gave her a dress-up tea party using the Cinderella theme. I provided all of the items mentioned earlier in this chapter. Some dresses I made at home and some were purchased from thrift stores.

The shoes used were re-cycled high heels in gold, silver, sequined, jeweled and beaded. Several pairs were children's plastic dress-up shoes purchased from toy stores. One thing to keep in mind when purchasing children's small sizes is those children's feet grow and usually after the age of five or six they don't fit. When purchasing used shoes, try to pick a medium heel. The three-inch heels tend to make the children trip and you don't want anyone hurt or ankles twisted.

Initially the girls chose the dresses they wanted to wear. After they were dressed, it was time to polish their nails. While the nails were drying, we did their makeup. It is such fun to watch these little darlings change when you apply their makeup. They immediately want to look into a mirror. Hmmm, does that ring a familiar note?

From the dressing room, the girls were directed to the craft area, where they made beaded necklaces or bracelets. They were given beads and cording, and created this project any way they wanted to. They were able to take this home with them as a keepsake. Instead of playing games at this type of party, choosing a craft instead can help keep things under control. When they finished their craft, the girls were called to the tea table, which was set ahead of time. The sandwich menu was the same as Alec's party. We did not have the gelatin shapes, but had baby carrots instead to be dipped in salad dressing.

A Princess story was read during their time at the table. The cake was fashioned like a Cinderella doll in Jordyn's favorite color, pink. The little girls oohed and ahhd when they saw it. Of course, children always enjoy cake and ice cream.

Now it was gift time. Before Jordyn opened any present, the gift giver took it to her and stayed next to her until it was opened. The contents were held up for everyone to see; then the guest and Jordyn smiled for a picture. Request double processing when getting the pictures developed. The mother will have an extra photo to enclose of the dressed up child in the thank you note. This works very well. No one has to write down the gifts received and the possibility of losing the paper, and the guest has a photo of herself with good memories of the party.

A year ago I was presented with another granddaughter named Tia. What blissful joy she is to me. I'm looking forward to the time we can sit at a tea table together with a wee set sipping tea and making memories of our own.

How About Boys?

Don't forget the boys, they enjoy teas too! Of course you wouldn't invite them to a dress-up and makeup party, but they would be happy to join the group in their "Sunday best" clothes. When they are under seven they enjoy the tea for what it is. In time they will learn to be gentlemen and serve the ladies, offer their arm and walk them to their places, and pull their chairs out for them to be seated. Now, isn't that good training? After the age of eight both girls and boys can start making scones, finger sandwiches, and many of the other simpler things that go along with the tea party. It is also a good time to teach them how to set the table correctly. Instruct them in the proper placement of the knife and fork, the water glass, and napkin. This etiquette is not exclusively for girls!

Cinnamon Bear Recipe

1 cup applesauce
1 1/2 cup cinnamon
1/3 cup glue

Mix all together into a ball and refrigerate one half hour. Roll out flat and cut into shapes—takes about 24 hours to dry.

Teddy Bear Cake

I have used this recipe several times over the years and it has always been bearable. Study the photograph before purchasing the ingredients. This is an easy-to-make cake.

1 box of cake mix
unsweetened chocolate
butter or margarine
angel flake coconut
large marshmallows
1 white mint
black licorice
brown cookies
red gumdrops
M & Ms
candy

Bake one 8-inch round and a 9-inch square cake. Cool. Cut square cake as shown and arrange the pieces on a tray or foil wrapped cutting board. Then place a marshmallow at the end of each paw.

Melt three squares of unsweetened chocolate and set aside 1/4 cup. Blend two tablespoons of butter/margarine into the remaining chocolate. Then stir two cups of coconut into butter-chocolate mixture. Chill.

Make your favorite frosting recipe. Save 1 1/3 cups white to frost Teddy's face and tummy, and marshmallow paws. Now carefully stir the chocolate you set aside into the remaining frosting and spread it over the rest of the cake. Sprinkle plain coconut over the white frosting and chocolate covered coconut over the chocolate frosting. Use cookies for his ears, and candies for his face, paws and tummy.

Chapter Seven

Hospitality and Tea Etiquette

"Do not neglect to show hospitality."

—Hebrews 13:2

Sharing Hospitality in the Home

*I*n the world in which we live, hospitality is a rare thing. Many people today aren't interested in reaching out to others and sharing what they have or taking the time to do it. Hospitality is a way of sharing your home, family, ideas, and extending yourself to others.

Even though our definition of hospitality and entertaining is far more casual today than it was in the past, people still appreciate being treated well. Behind each set of eyes is a person like you with feelings. Treat each one with courtesy and respect.

In this chapter I will be discussing some biblical mandates to hospitality and what it means. Hospitality is different than entertaining. Entertaining is to show that we can put on a nice party, or that we have a lovely home and fabulous things. The focus is on us to impress, not to serve. That is called pride and there is no room for that, people are more important than things. People before pride—do you know what that means? Pride is when we brag about what a great meal we made, or the lovely china we used, and on and on. Those are things. We don't all have the same means to entertain; nonetheless, it is called home. It is where God has put us at this particular time and we are to use it for His glory. Hospitality is not to impress others but to serve them. Hebrews 13:2 tells us, "Do not neglect to show hospitality." Have a mindset like Jesus, and have a servant's heart. That is what it requires to be a servant of all.

What is the purpose of hospitality? Christians are commanded to practice hospitality; it is an effective means for evangelism. We may be the only Bible that people "see". It is to share what you have with others and an exchange of fellowship and love. Romans 12:13 says, "contributing to the needs of the saints, practicing hospitality." Basically, the meaning is mutual sharing, not just with friends, but also with strangers. "Be hospitable to one another without complaint," also refers to hospitality shown to strangers (1 Peter 4:9). "It is the friendly, generous reception of guests or strangers."

To share hospitality, the proper mindset is of utmost importance. Show a good attitude and enthusiasm for what you are going to be involved in. Make your guests feel comfortable; kindness is always appreciated. "Blessed are those who can give without remembering, and take without forgetting" (Elizabeth Bibesco).

When your guests arrive, try to greet each one at the door and make them feel welcome, "I'm so glad you were able to come today Dulcie, let's go meet some of the other guests." Be sure everyone gets introduced and doesn't feel left out. If you happen to be involved in getting things prepared, ask someone if they would answer the door for you momentarily. Have a few pop questions to throw out if the conversation is lacking; sometimes that's all it takes to get things going. As a suggestion, ask the following: "Is the tea that's used in tea bags inferior to tea that is bought loose, or specialty teas you can buy in gourmet shops?" True or false? Another one, "Iced tea was invented by an Englishman in the 1800s as a new beverage for the aristocracy" True or false? (It would be nice if you knew the answers; they are both false.)

When it is time for the guests to leave, see each one to the door and tell them how much you appreciate them giving their time to be with you, and how good it was to see them again. "Please, let's keep in touch," you say.

One of the sweet young seminary wives in our church wanted to know everything there was about opening her home. She would go to various seasoned women of the church who displayed different gifts, and learn from them. She then put everything she learned into practice.

Near Valentine's Day one of the dearest things she does is plan a Valentine Pampering Party for those ladies that don't have as much as some. Vicki would call ladies in January that have some experience with hair styling, massage, nail care, facials and makeup. One year I did draping of colors for the young women.

We volunteered our time from about 11:00 A.M. to 2:00 P.M., and the guests were able to come any time that was convenient for them to get pampered. Their children were even able to join them. While mom was relaxing and getting beautified, Vicki would take the children into the back yard and play games with them, or sit on a blanket and do hand action songs. It was such a precious thing to observe. In the kitchen were choices of both hot and cold beverages and various finger foods on the table for eating. Vicki learned quickly the importance of investing time in others and how to best exemplify the Proverbs 31 woman.

In her book, *Open Heart Open Home*, Karen Mains states, "I am convinced that true hospitality will only flower if our homes are open to each other." To give our lives away to others is the most fulfilling, fruitful objective we can have.

Preparing Your Time Table

In order to have a successful tea gathering there needs to be a plan. "Teach us to number our days aright, that we may gain a heart of wisdom" (Psalm 90:12). As you are forming ideas as to when, how many, and where all of this is going to take place, start jotting those ideas down. When you decide on a date, make an organized chart using the following guidelines!

- *One month before the event:* purchase or make invitations. Don't forget the stamps.

- *Three weeks before:* send out invitations with R.S.V.P., or Regrets Only (specify date) five days before the event.

- *Two weeks before:* start doing the hard tasks first. Polishing silver, cleaning the refrigerator, washing windows, and other chores. Colossians 3:23 says, "Whatever you do, work at it with all your heart, as working for the Lord, not for men."

- *One week before:* make out your menu and purchase as much in advance as possible. You can make your scones and pecan tassies now and put them in the freezer. Select and prepare linens. Start doing general house cleaning.

- *Three days before:* choose teapots, cups and saucers, serving plates. Make lemon curd. Select music for the tea.

- *Day before:* get the house ship-shape and set the tea table. Purchase and arrange the flowers. Prepare the English trifle and the sandwiches.

❧ *The morning of the party:* PRAY. Have a nice bath or shower. Above all, be relaxed so you can be a lovely hostess for your guests. Get dressed, do your makeup, comb your hair, and you are prepared for the remainder of the day. When we are servants, our hospitality takes on a different dimension.

❧ *One hour before:* get the tea equipment ready, put sandwiches on serving dishes and cover with a damp cloth so they don't dry out. The sweets are now to be displayed on a buffet table. Don't forget the tassies in the freezer. Have as much out and ready to go as possible so you are not pressured at the last minute. Place paper doilies on each serving plate, as this will definitely dress up the table.

❧ *Thirty minutes before:* pop the frozen scones in the oven and any other frozen items you might be having that need baking, such as mini quiches.

❧ *Fifteen minutes before:* plug in electric teakettle to keep the water hot and ready for use. Give a last minute check on everything. Now you are ready to receive your guests. Before you seat the ladies, remove the damp cloths from the sandwiches. Enjoy your time!

When it is all over, make notes as to what you might do different next time or what was the best thing that happened. There is a lady I know that has folders on every party she has ever given, with complete notes from start to finish! Starting with the invitation, guest list, menu, comments from guests, even the weather. You never know when you might have to move a party indoors. That is organization. Going back over notes always gives you new ways to improve your skills, or use the ones that worked the first time.

Out and About Hospitality

One of my favorite ways to show hospitality away from my home is to take a tea basket to strangers, as well as friends. I call this "Teacups to Go." A few years ago at a Christian Women's Club luncheon a pastor's wife spoke on this very thing. I said to myself, "I can do that." Since that time I have often put it into practice.

There have been many opportunities to teach this concept to small groups at community colleges, seminars, and ladies at my church to encourage them to reach out in this way.

The first thing you will need is a good sized wicker basket, two cups and saucers, two napkins, a tea plate for sweets, spoons, a tea pot, and a Thermos to carry hot water. The reason for supplying the hot water is that you don't want the person that you are visiting to have to do anything but be coddled and to enjoy the moment. Now, add a candle (don't forget the matches), a small vase to hold either an artificial or fresh flower, a wee cosmetic bag to hold two tea bags, packaged sweetener and creamer. The bag keeps things tidy. The last item is the tea cloth, which is draped over the basket. Now you're ready to go, so let's put it into practice.

Let's use this scenario: a new neighbor has moved in and you haven't met her yet. Pray first, pick up your basket, and go to the neighbor's. Ring the doorbell "Hello, I'm Nan Taylor and I live across the street. I would like to welcome you into the neighborhood. Do you have a few minutes for a cup of tea?" That's all there is to it. When the neighbor invites you in and shows you where you can visit, start opening the basket.

Place the tea cloth first on the table, and each item thereafter. When we are about to start our tea party, I ask if I can read "A Teatime Blessing." She always says yes. "Lord, grant that our time together be steeped in serenity, sweetened by sharing, and surrounded by the warm fragrance of Your love, Amen" (taken from *If Teacups Could Talk*, by Emilie Barnes). That little prayer opens the door to talk of things of the Lord if she is a believer. If there is no interest in spiritual things, the topic is changed and you go from there. Hopefully you have touched that woman's heart.

About thirty minutes is enough time for this experience. You can learn a lot about your new neighbor in that time. She will be so amazed and touched by the fact that you gave your time and truly showed you cared; what an example of Christ. I also leave a copy of "A Teatime Blessing," which was printed on my computer on card stock. One can also visit friends in nursing homes, as well as new moms, the bereaved, and those who have recently had surgery and returned home from a stay in the hospital. It is thoughtful to take a meal as well. Doesn't this sound like a wonderful ministry for you?

This could also be incorporated into a romantic picnic under a sprawling tree with your loved one, an evening on the terrace with a full moon above, in front of a blazing fire on a cold winter night, or what have you. It's a perfect way to share cherished moments with that someone special.

I keep my basket packed and ready to go at a moments notice. Hot water, sweets and a fresh flower is all that has to be added.

> *The crown of the home is Godliness,*
> *The beauty of the home is order,*
> *The blessing of the home is contentment,*
> *The glory of the home is hospitality.*

> —Old Inscription

Tea Etiquette

What is "etiquette?" Etiquette is a fancy word for simple kindness. In other words, getting along with others in a polite way. The rules of etiquette are called "manners." We are most familiar with this term. She has good manners; we'll invite her again. Or, the child wasn't taught any manners and therefore was annoying to be around. Does that sound a bit like today's world? Manners are what make you feel confident in any situation. It is uncomfortable to be somewhere and look around to see what everyone else is doing and wonder if you are out of place, or exactly who is doing the proper thing. Hopefully, after this section of the book you will know and have that confidence to go anywhere, anytime.

Manners are definitely an attitude of having a kinder, gentler heart, being thoughtful and considerate of others. Learning the rules of etiquette helps focus on making others comfortable. Manners boil down to the Golden Rule: "And just as you want people to treat you, treat them in the same way" (Luke 6:31). Manners prevent us from being selfish or annoying. They make us better company and a better person.

The Invitation

First we will start with the invitation. When you receive an invitation, it is desirable to respond quickly. The person who sent the invitation has to plan on food, seating arrangements and many other details. If you are unable to attend, tell the hostess your regrets and wish her a successful tea party. You would want the same courtesies shown you.

The Event

Once you have accepted the invitation, *be on time*. Upon arrival, greet your hostess first. Extend your gratefulness for the invitation with a hostess remembrance. Try not to take too much of her time as she has many things on her mind. Mingle with the other guests and introduce yourself to those you don't know. This is how you make yourself known, and new acquaintances can in turn, learn something about you. We are so secure talking to those we are already familiar with; oftentimes we do not receive the blessing of meeting new friends or expanding our horizons by reaching out to others.

A good introduction includes our first and last name. For example: "Hello, I'm Nan Taylor, I know Jane from Bible study." That tells the other person your name, how you know the hostess, and that you go to a Bible study. Be a considerate guest and introduce people you know to one another.

If the event is an open buffet, help yourself to the food. Put a small amount on the tea plate provided. You can always go back for more. Get a cup of tea and continue mingling. This is a great way to meet others and improve your greeting and conversational skills.

It is a bit awkward to try to sip tea and eat with both hands busy. Set your teacup and saucer on a side table, and eat your sandwiches. Take at least two bites per sandwich. With small bites, it allows you to be able to answer any questions. When you are ready for your tea, lift both the cup and saucer to about chest level; raise the cup to your lips and take a sip of tea. As mentioned earlier in this book, avoid separating the cup from the saucer that is more than twelve inches from your mouth.

You may return for tea and food as often as you wish. Once you have finished eating, place the cup, saucer and tea plate on a side table that has been designated for that purpose, never back on the tea-serving table.

If you are attending a sit-down tea with assigned seating, approach your chair entering from your left side. Pull the chair away from the table far enough so that you may slide in gently and not bump it. Ease yourself into the chair gracefully, using your legs to lower your body. Once your bottom is in the chair, raise your body, grasp the sides of the chair, and slide up to the table. Place the napkin on your lap with the fold facing your body. Use it to dab the corners of your mouth gently. Please don't wipe your lipstick on it. The napkin stays on your lap until you are completely finished and ready to leave, then it should be placed on the table, not folded. If you need to leave the table during the meal, place the napkin on your chair, indicating you're returning. When you are finished and leaving, remember to glide up from the chair slowly and gracefully, just as you entered it. Push the chair back under table.

Most often the food as well as the tea will be on the table. Make an effort to meet each person at your table. Be friendly, as it puts everyone at ease.

The table hostess pours the tea and you serve yourself the food. If an item is out of reach, ask politely; "Please pass the scones, Mary." Of course, I know you will remember not to chew with your mouth open or smack your lips. As commented on earlier, take small bites; you will find it easier to respond if someone asks you questions. That can't be stated enough. Wait until you have swallowed the food in your mouth before taking a sip of tea. Choking makes everyone uncomfortable. When drinking your tea, look into the cup, not over it. This will control any accidental spills or embarrassment. If sugar is added for sweetness, stir in a small circular motion in the center of the cup, so as not to tinkle the sides and make a noise.

> *"We live in stirring times, tea*
> *stirring times."*
> —Christopher Isherwood

Often the desserts will be placed on a buffet table. Feel free to partake of them when you are finished with the sandwich course. Where will you leave your napkin when going to the buffet table? On the chair!

Most tea parties last about two hours, sometimes a bit longer. Don't over-stay your welcome. One of my mother's favorite sayings after finishing a meal was, "I've had an elegant sufficiency thank you." Find your hostess and thank her for a wonderful party and your sufficiency, then make your exit. After you have said your farewell, don't linger around talking to your friends. That keeps them from leaving at an appropriate time. When the party is over, leave.

Thank-You Notes

Should I send a thank-you note? Absolutely, don't let this one slip by. Our society today has gotten so blasé that we miss the most important things. In your note thank the hostess for inviting you and let her know how much you enjoyed the other guests. Give her a compliment either on the food, decorations, or something else you might have noticed or enjoyed at the tea. Above all, send this out within 24 hours after attending the event. It will still be fresh in your memory and won't haunt you that it hasn't been done.

Tea Rooms

If you and a friend are going to a tearoom, use the same tea etiquette outlined in this chapter. Here are a couple of other pointers:

Most women like to take their handbag with them wherever they go. I'm not sure if this is because they have so much money they are protecting their wallet, or if it is for refreshing their makeup. Personally, I think it is a like a security blanket. Whatever the reason, do not put your handbag on the table. This rule of thumb extends to keys, hats, eyeglasses or anything that is not part of the meal. Place purses on the floor, near or under your chair.

If something gets stuck in your teeth, don't try to remove it in the presence of others. Excuse yourself and use the rest room.

Before you go out with a friend, discuss who is going to pay the bill. If you have done the inviting, then don't involve your guest in paying the bill. If you are the guest, then graciously accept the gesture, and be sure to send a thank you note.

Sometimes you will go with a group for tea. Either divide the bill evenly or have someone pay by credit card and collect from each person after leaving the tearoom. Don't make this a conspicuous ordeal.

Please, please, please always wear a dress or skirt to any tea function. We are so fortunate to be women, so delight in it. Taking tea is different from any other ritual that you might attend. Give it your finest attention. It is so feminine, and it builds one's confidence by looking their best. In her book, *The Fragrance of Beauty*, Joyce Landorf says, "Pray that the fragrance of God's beauty will enfold and surround your entire being." 1 Peter 3:4 says, "Be beautiful inside your hearts, with the lasting charm of the gentle and quiet spirit which is so precious to God."

Bring warmth, enthusiasm and unrestricted joy into any room, simply by the way you walk into it. Learn to walk tall, confident, and poised. It's making the best of the original you that God designed and created; our lives do speak to others.

> *"One of life's greatest treasures*
> *That God in His goodness sends,*
> *Is the love that binds hearts together,*
> *In the covenant known as friends."*
>
> —Roy Lessin

Chapter Eight

Invitations and Party Favors

Guess Who's Coming to Tea?

Creative invitations can be made in a variety of ways using an assortment of textures and paper products. There are so many pretty papers available that it's hard to choose which is best for the occasion. Purchasing invitations is another possibility or you can have them professionally printed.

In this chapter I have outlined a few simple suggestions for making your own invitations. I am sure you can use these ideas if you so desire. It is always more enjoyable if two or more are gathered together, so have fun making them and involve a friend if possible.

Some of the papers that may be used for invitations can be purchased directly from a paper company or large paper warehouses. If you do not have that convenience in your area, a variety of papers can be ordered through the mail from a paper catalog or over the Internet. Be creative and you will find something suitable.

Now as for me, when I receive an invitation in the mail it sends a rush of adrenaline. I open the envelope as quickly as possible to see what is on the inside. After I have read the content with excitement, then I take time to enjoy the creativity of the invitation. Whether it be made by the sender's hands or purchased, a lot of thought and preparation went into it. A habit I have formed is to go directly to the calendar to see if the date and time are a possibility and respond to the sender as soon as possible. It is not good practice to ignore the invitation, as she will be inconvenienced if you don't respond.

Party favors are not a requirement, but they are enjoyed and appreciated by those who attend your event. For me, it is exciting and fun to plan on what type of favor I will make for my guests. After I have decided on what the project is going to be, going out and purchasing the supplies is a treasure hunt. It is important to put thought and consideration into each gift whether it is hand crafted or purchased for the upcoming occasion.

Invitation Suggestions

Suggestion One

Use a 5 x 7 sheet of textured, deckle edge paper and fold in half. Cut a 4" paper doily in half and glue one half of it onto the front side of the paper. Choose a lovely sticker and place in the middle of the doily. The sticker can be a rose, Victorian girl, baby or whatever your theme might be. Add a ribbon and tie in a bow. On the inside of the folded paper, glue the pre-printed or typed invitation, following this example.

❧

You are invited to a farewell gathering for

Jordyn Kelsey

Tea will be served at one o'clock in the afternoon
on Friday, January 8, 2004
at 12345 Gunther Street, Pleasant Town

Please bring one of your favorite teacups and saucer

Regrets only:
Jane Austin (555) 123-4567
Lindy Jones (555) 789-0123

❧

Suggestion Two

Use a 5 1/2 x 8 1/2 sheet of thin paper and fold in half. Type your text or have it professionally printed. Another possibility is to have someone write it out using calligraphy. Whatever you choose, place the text on the inside bottom half of the paper. On the outside front, on the diagonal glue a piece of Moiré ribbon, pointed in the corners toward the card. On top of the ribbon, glue a lace flower. Very elegant.

Suggestion Three

Invitation to a baby shower: Use a piece of 4 1/4 x 5 1/4 white card stock. Take a piece of pink letter stock paper 4 1/4 x 5 1/4. Cut the both the white and pink papers together with scalloped scissors, just the sides. Stamp the pink paper with baby rattles or whatever the theme is. This happens to be for a girl baby shower. Use any pastel paper and stamp that will emphasize your theme. Purchase some vellum and cut 4 x 5 sheets. Using the same scalloped scissors, trim on all four sides. Have your message printed on the vellum, starting a minimum of 1" from the top. Center the printed vellum on the other two pieces of paper. With a hole punch, punch two holes not quite 1/2" from the top. Thread 1/4" satin or organdy ribbon from the back to the front and tie in front; cut a "V" on the ends of the ribbon.

The message on this particular invitation could read as follows:

~

The pleasure of your company is requested
In celebrating the arrival of

Tia Rianne Taylor

Tea will be served at 10 o'clock in the morning
on Friday, January 8, 2000
at 12345 Pine Ridge, Pleasant Town

Please R.S.V.P
Gloria Smith (555) 246-8024

~

Suggestion Four

Hand-stamped invitations: With the craft of stamping, you can use a variety of stamps to decorate the front of your invitation. Use the same motif on the place cards for your table. Use a heavy card stock, cut 5 1/2" x 8 1/2" and fold in half. Use decorative scissors to trim the front lower flap edge. It will be a bit shorter than the inside back. Then, stamp, stamp, stamp, to your hearts content.

Suggestion Five
Invitation to a tea bridal shower:

～

The pleasure of your company is requested
At a tea in celebration of

Alec Bender
For her upcoming marriage.

Please join us on Saturday, the twenty-eighth of March,
Two thousand and twenty, at two o'clock in the afternoon
At the home of
Barbara Mayes
12345 Oak Dale St., Pleasant Town

Come dressed in Victorian flair as your wardrobe allows

Kindly reply:
Joyce (555) 135-7913
or Beth (555) 234-5678

～

Party Favors Ideas

Teacup Lamp–The Light of the World
Supplies:

- ❧ cup and saucer
- ❧ glue that will bond glass or china
- ❧ battery operated candlestick
- ❧ small paper or cloth lampshade
- ❧ Styrofoam
- ❧ Spanish moss
- ❧ greenery and flower

Note: Now is the time to start canvassing yard sales, thrift shops and the like for inexpensive cups and saucers. If there is a chip in the cup, it doesn't matter because you will be able to cover it up with greenery. The cups may not match with the saucers, but if there is a close resemblance it makes an interesting set.

Purchase a battery operated candlestick and a paper lampshade that will fit the bulb of the candlestick after you have chosen your cup and saucer. Many craft stores carry these types of candlesticks.

How to Assemble

Glue cup to saucer. Glue candlestick inside of the cup. Gather some Styrofoam, Spanish moss, greenery and flowers. Break up Styrofoam so it will fit in cup snugly and cover with Spanish moss. Use household glue to arrange greenery and flowers in the cup.

When everything has dried, add the lampshade. This makes a great decoration in a dimly lit spot, in the bathroom, or on a shelf and can also be a much appreciated gift. I have used two or three on a tea table when having guests. Don't forget the 2-AA batteries.

Teacup Candle

Here is another fun item to make while you are out collecting inexpensive cups and saucers.

Supplies:

- cup and saucer
- glass and china glue
- paraffin wax
- candlewick, wick tabs (to hold the wick in place)
- old crayons or candles for color

You can also buy color as well as fragrance at most craft stores if you want something unusual. For smaller projects like this I prefer paraffin instead of candle wax because it's less expensive. A large block of candle wax might be more economical if you plan on using a lot or share it with a friend. Another option is the new candle gels that are available.

How to Assemble

Glue cup to saucer with glass or china glue. Take a pan of water and a coffee can that will fit inside. Use the coffee can to melt the wax. (Be careful not to have the flame of the fire too high.) While the water is coming to a slow boil and the wax is beginning to melt, cut a piece of candlewick to fit just above the rim of the cup. Attach to the wick tab. Place in the teacup. The more candles you can make at one time the better. It will take about 24 hours to set up. There will be a well in the middle where the wax has shrunk. Melt more wax and pour slowly just to fill the well and to get a smooth surface. These are great for birthday gifts or any other occasion.

Decorated Styrofoam Hat

Supplies:

- ❧ 10 ounce Styrofoam cups

- ❧ bits and pieces of lace, fabric, flowers, jewelry

- ❧ fabric paint of your color choice and pearl or white paint

- ❧ paint brush and household glue or hot glue

- ❧ plastic tubs for paint

How to Assemble

In a 450° oven, place three or four Styrofoam cups on a cookie sheet. Bake for approximately 10 to 12 seconds, they will melt into hat shapes. Since oven heating temperatures vary, you should watch these carefully. If you can see through your oven door window, watch to see if 12 seconds is the right time. You may need to add a second or two more for a complete melt down. It's fun to watch those little things melt into shapes of hats.

As a precaution, while in the melting process I suggest you put on a mask or something over your nose and mouth as the toxic fumes are pretty strong. Open windows and doors to allow fumes to escape. Remove from the oven and put in three or four more to bake. Start mixing paint when you have enough hats. Add some white or pearl paint to the colored paint to give an interesting texture. Paint both inside and out.

When completely dry, start applying all of the bits and pieces you have gathered and watch the hats come alive. See, you knew you were saving those pieces and snippets for something! You might want to add a pin back so it can be used as a darling broach.

Sweet Bonnet Cookie

Supplies:

- ♪ purchase 2-3/4" round cookies, preferably with scalloped edges
- ♪ 1 box of Vanilla Wafers
- ♪ small plastic bag and ribbon, to tie as package
- ♪ pastry bag for icing
- ♪ star tip #16 for flowers
- ♪ round tip #3 for flower center
- ♪ flat tip #47 for band and ribbon
- ♪ food coloring plastic tubs for different colored icing

How to Assemble

Make your icing and divide into plastic tubs.

Leave some white, some blue, pink, green or whatever colors you choose using food coloring. The icing becomes the glue. Place a Vanilla Wafer or two in the center for each round cookie and glue in place. Decorate hats with icing pumped through pastry bags. (As mentioned above, use star tip for flowers, round tip for center of flowers, flat tip for ribbons and hatband.)

When icing has hardened, place each cookie in a plastic bag and tie with a ribbon. These freeze well and can be made in advance.

Sachet Tea Bag

Supplies:

- ♪ white see thru fabric such as organza, medium weight
- ♪ 1/8" ribbon
- ♪ small fabric satin roses
- ♪ potpourri
- ♪ white paper card stock

How to Assemble

Cut fabric 7" long by 5" wide. Fold long edges together. Sew or glue seam together, making 1/8" seam. You now have a long tube. On the seam side, pinch about 1/8" in center and fold sides to top, toward the front. You now have two open ends with a crease in the middle, like a flow thru tea bag. On both sides, put about 1 tablespoon of potpourri in each opening. Make a small double fold over the top and staple shut. Glue a 5" strip of 1/8" ribbon over staple and a satin rose over the ribbon. From a small piece of card stock, cut two pieces identical in size and shape for the name of the guest, or name of the potpourri fragrance. Be creative. Glue the pieces together with the ribbon sandwiched in between.

Felt Diaper Nut Cup

These are so cute for baby showers.

Supplies:

- ❧ 2 each 9 x 12" pink and blue felt squares
- ❧ small gold safety pins
- ❧ paraffin wax
- ❧ nuts and mints

How to Assemble

Cut each diaper into a 6 x 6 x 5 3/4" triangle. With point of triangle pointing down, fold tip of felt toward the top and fold each side over to the middle, overlapping slightly, just enough to pin layers together. Pin through all layers. Put a pan of water on to boil. When the water reaches the boiling point, reduce heat. Carefully place a block of paraffin in a clean one-pound coffee can. Place the coffee can gently in the boiling water.

When the paraffin is melted, take a pair of kitchen tongs and dip the felt diaper into the wax. Cover the entire diaper, and drain wax completely. Place diaper on wax paper to cool. Sit diaper on its bottom so it will stand up. Make as many as you need and fill either with nuts or mints. Your guests will be crazy about them them.

Chapter Nine

Making Scones and Other Tea Related Recipes

"Busy Hands are Happy Hands"

—An Old Adage

*H*ow could one possibly have a tea without recipes? These are just a few of my treasured ones. Some are from friends in England, Australia and New Zealand. There are a myriad of books on the market with wonderful recipes in them, but that is not what this book is about. Do enjoy the ones that are offered here.

Scones

The classic scone is like a blank canvas: simple, unadorned, and ready to be spread with butter, jam, lemon curd, or clotted cream.

> *2 cups flour*
> *2 teaspoons baking powder*
> *2 tablespoons sugar*
> *1/2 teaspoon salt*
> *1/4 cup butter, room temp*
> *2 eggs, slightly beaten*
> *1/2 to 3/4 cup heavy whipping cream or buttermilk*

Preheat oven to 400°. Mix the first four ingredients in a large bowl. With a pastry cutter work in the butter until the mixture is crumbly. Work in the eggs and cream or buttermilk, adjusting until mixture is tender and moist but not runny. Drop the dough by generous 1/4 cup portions onto a greased cookie sheet or turn onto lightly floured surface and knead into a circle about 3/4" thick; then cut into wedges and place wedges on cookie sheet. Bake at 400° for 15 minutes or until scones are golden in color. Scones may be made a day before and stored in airtight containers, but are at their best served fresh and warm. Yield: 12 scones.

Variations

After adding the eggs and cream or buttermilk, you can stir any of the following into your scones: 1/2 cup dried, fresh, or thawed frozen blueberries and 2 teaspoons fresh lemon zest; 1/2 cup chocolate chips and 1 teaspoon vanilla; 1/2 cup dried currants or raisins with 1/4 teaspoon cinnamon; or 1/2 cup dried cranberries or cherries and 1/4 cup chopped pecans, or just 1/4 cup walnuts.

Cheese Scones

These little scones make a delightful savory. Serve them warm, split and lightly buttered.

> *1 1/2 cups self-rising flour*
> *2 tablespoons margarine*
> *1/2 cup cheddar cheese, grated*
> *pinch of salt*
> *pinch of cayenne*
> *1 egg, slightly beaten*
> *a little milk*

Put the flour and margarine into the food processor and process until the mixture resembles coarse breadcrumbs. Add the cheese, salt and cayenne and process to mix—just a few seconds. With the machine on add the egg, together with just enough milk to make soft, pliable dough. Roll out on a lightly floured board and cut into rounds using a pastry cutter. Place on greased baking sheet, brush with beaten egg, and bake for about 20 minutes at 425°.

Cranberry-Orange Scones

> *1 3/4 cup all purpose flour*
> *1/2 teaspoon allspice*
> *3 tablespoons sugar*
> *1/2 teaspoon salt*
> *2 1/2 teaspoons baking powder*
> *5 tablespoons unsalted butter, chilled, cut into pieces*
> *1/2 cup dried cranberries*
> *6 tablespoons half and half*
> *1 large egg, beaten to blend*
> *2 tablespoons orange peel*

In medium size mixing bowl, sift together the dry ingredients then add the butter, cutting in until the mixture resembles coarse meal. Stir in cranberries.

In a separate bowl, whisk together the half-and-half, egg, and orange peel. Add this mixture to the dry mixture and stir until the dough just comes together. Transfer it to a lightly floured work surface, then knead a couple of times and shape into a 1/2" thick round. Cut the round in half and each half into 5 wedges. Separate the wedges and transfer them to a nonstick, parchment-lined, or lightly greased baking sheet. Bake the scones in a preheated oven at 400° for about 10 minutes or until golden brown. Yield: 10 scones. You may brush the tops with some milk and sprinkle with cinnamon sugar.

Pecan Tassies

2–3 ounces cream cheese
2 cubes butter or margarine
2 cups flour

Blend softened cream cheese and butter together, then add flour. Knead ingredients into soft dough and chill.

Filling

3 eggs
2 cups brown sugar (packed)
3 tablespoons soft butter
2 teaspoons vanilla
1 teaspoon salt
1 1/3 cups chopped pecans

Mix filling together and assemble as follows. Pinch off small pieces of dough and roll into small balls, then press into miniature muffin pans sprayed with cooking spray. Add filing and bake at 350° for 20 to 25 minutes. Cool for about 10 minutes, remove from pans, and sprinkle with powdered sugar when completely cool. Yield: 42

Lemon Curd

1/2 cube butter (1/4 cup)
1 3/4 cups sugar
1/2 cups lemon juice
4 eggs, beaten
2 tablespoons lemon peel
dash of salt

In double boiler over boiling water add the above ingredients. Whisk or stir mixture until it thickens, about 10 minutes. Don't stop stirring or you'll have scrambled eggs. Guess how I know? The curd should be the consistency of sour cream. Makes one pint and can be stored in refrigerator up to a month. For a change this also tastes great using orange juice and peel.

Mock Clotted Cream

3 ounces cream cheese, softened
1 cup whipping cream
1 teaspoon confectioner's sugar
dash of vanilla

Blend all ingredients in a food processor or with a mixer until thick. Serve with scones instead of butter.

Mock Devonshire Cream

1 cup whipping or heavy cream
1 cup sour cream
4 tablespoons confectioner's sugar

Beat cream until medium stiff peaks form, adding sugar in the last few minutes of mixing. Fold in the sour cream and blend well. Refrigerate. Serve with scones instead of butter.

English Trifle

1/2 pint whipping cream
3 tablespoons sugar
1/4 teaspoon vanilla
1 angel food or sponge cake
1 large instant vanilla pudding
strawberries
1 banana or other fruit in season
slivered almonds

With electric mixer beat whipping cream until stiff, add 3 tablespoons sugar and 1/4 teaspoon vanilla near end of beating. Set aside. In trifle bowl break up about 2/3 of the cake into small pieces and put 1/2 on bottom of bowl, add 1/2 pudding, slice strawberries and decorate side of bowl with inside of strawberry showing through bowl. Slice banana and put on top of pudding and any other fruit you might be using. Add whipped cream and layer again. Cover top of trifle with remaining whipping cream and sprinkle slivered almonds, strawberries and any other fruit you might be using. Refrigerate until serving time. Yummy! Can be made 24 hours ahead.

Cheese Tarts

3 8 ounce-packages cream cheese
3 eggs
3/4 cup sugar
1 teaspoon vanilla extract
1 teaspoon lemon juice
1 box vanilla wafers

Put whole vanilla wafer in foil cupcake cups. Blend filling. Pour into cups about 1/2 full. Bake at 375° for 15 minutes. Cool. Top with favorite topping or any canned pie filling such as strawberry, cherry or blueberry.

The Great New Zealand Pavlova

This New Zealand national dessert was sent to me from Edna Pearson. It's a crisp shell of meringue with a marshmallow center is topped with whipped cream and fruit.

> *4 egg whites*
> *few grains salt*
> *3/4 cup granulated sugar*
> *1/2 teaspoon vanilla extract*
> *1 teaspoon vinegar*
> *1 teaspoon cornstarch*

Preheat oven to 350°. (The temperature is reduced for baking.) Place a sheet of parchment paper on a baking sheet. Brush lightly with melted butter and dust with a little cornstarch; shake off excess. Beat the egg whites to a foam with a rotary or electric beater. Add the salt. Beat to a stiff foam or until the peaks fold over when the beater is removed. Beat in the sugar 1 tablespoon at a time; continue beating until mixture is stiff and the peaks stand stiff. Add the vanilla, vinegar and cornstarch. Blend thoroughly. Spoon the meringue mixture onto prepared cookie sheet, forming a 9-inch circle. On lower rack of oven, bake at 275° for 15 minutes, then reduce to 250° for 1 to 1 1/4 hours. Allow to cool in oven. Place on a flat serving dish. Pile with whipped cream on top, spreading out in swirls. Decorate with fruit; kiwi, strawberries or bananas. Or any fruit of you choice.

Anzac Cookies

Bronwen Cox sent me this Australian favorite! The acronym ANZAC stands for Australian and New Zealand Army Corps. The first "A" stands for Australia, the "NZ" for New Zealand and "AC" for Army Corps. They served together in World War I at Gallipoli in Turkey and were renowned for bravery. Both countries still celebrate Anzac Day on the 25th of April every year.

> *1 cup rolled oats (not quick or instant oats)*
> *1 cup brown sugar, firmly packed*
> *1 cup all purpose flour*
> *1/2 cup coconut*
> *4 ounces butter*
> *2 1/2 tablespoons honey*
> *1/2 teaspoon baking soda*
> *1 tablespoon water*
> *almonds for decoration*

Combine oats, brown sugar, flour, and coconut in large bowl. Place butter, water and honey in a microwave-proof bowl and microwave for 1 minute, or until butter is melted. Stir baking soda into liquid mixture, it will become foamy, and then add to the dry ingredients. If mixture does not hold together, add a few drops of water at a time until it holds a form. Place rounded teaspoons of dough two inches apart on a lightly greased baking sheet or use parchment paper. Put one slivered or whole almond on top of each cookie and bake at 350° for 15 minutes or until slightly firm. They will become crisper as they cool. Makes 25

Lamingtons

Another wonderful recipe from my friends down under. Purchase a day old sponge or pound cake. Cut into 2 x 2" squares and coat with the following.

Chocolate Icing

2 cups powdered sugar
1 tablespoon boiling water
1 tablespoon vanilla extract
1 tablespoon cocoa
1 1/2 cups shredded coconut

To prepare icing, sift powdered sugar into medium mixing bowl. In a separate bowl, combine the boiling water with the vanilla extract and the cocoa. Add the blended cocoa mixture to the powdered sugar and mix well. Ice the cake squares on all sides and roll in the coconut. Allow to dry on a wire rack. Store in an airtight container for up to a week, or serve right away.

Frosted Grapes

2 egg whites
large bunch of seedless grapes
sugar

Whisk the egg whites very lightly, being careful not to let a lot of bubbles form. Cut your large bunch of grapes into manageable small clusters. Using a brush, coat the grapes with egg whites. Then place the grapes in a shallow dish and pour sugar over them. Gently roll the grapes in the sugar to coat them completely. These make a beautiful presentation.

Haystacks

2 eggs
4 ounces sugar
12 ounces coconut

Beat egg, add sugar and beat again, stir in coconut. Mold into eggcups and tap out on greased cookie sheet. Bake 350° for 20 minutes or until golden. Yield: 16. If you don't have glass eggcups, you can use the plastic eggs that are available at Easter. You can also tint your coconut with food coloring. Fun for kids to make.

Banana Ball Surprise

Cut banana into six or eight pieces. Roll in lemon juice, drain on paper towel. Dip in sour cream and roll in shredded coconut. Refrigerate on cookie sheet for several hours. Yummy! One banana serves two people.

Brown Bread Ice Cream

The distinctive "nutty" flavor of this ice cream makes it very popular with adults as well as children. Traditionally English, it's delicious served with fresh summer fruits.

1 1/4 cup heavy cream
2/3 cup half and half
6 tablespoons confectioners sugar
2 cups brown breadcrumbs
2 eggs
1 tablespoon rum (or artificial flavor)

Beat the heavy cream until stiff, and then gradually beat in the half-and-half. Fold in the sugar and breadcrumbs. Separate the eggs, mix the yolks with the rum, and fold into ice cream mixture. Beat the egg whites until stiff and fold into the mixture. Pour into freezing trays or plastic container and freeze until firm.

Banana-Walnut Loaf

This is a lovely moist cake that keeps well. It is eaten sliced, with or without butter.

> *1/2 cup margarine*
> *3/4 cup dark brown sugar*
> *2 ripe bananas*
> *2 eggs*
> *2 1/4 cups self rising flour*
> *1 tablespoon baking powder*
> *1/2 cup chopped walnuts*
> *2 tablespoons milk*

Grease and line a one-pound loaf pan or 2 one-pound pans. Preheat oven to 350°. Cream margarine and sugar together. Mash bananas and add to the mixture. Break the eggs one at a time into the mixture, beating well between each addition. Gently fold in the flour and baking powder, stir in the walnuts and milk. Transfer the mixture into the loaf pan, smoothing the top, and bake for approximately one hour, or until well-risen and golden brown. Turn out and cool on a wire rack.

Victorian Poppy Seed Cake with Lime Syrup

> *1 cup unsalted butter, room temperature*
> *1 cup sour cream*
> *1 cup sugar*
> *4 egg yolks*
> *4 egg whites, stiffly beaten*
> *1 teaspoon almond extract*
> *1/4 cup poppy seed*
> *1 teaspoon vanilla extract*
> *2 cups cake flour*
> *1 teaspoon cinnamon*
> *1 teaspoon baking soda*

Preheat oven to 350°. Grease and flour a 10" tube pan. Cream butter, sugar, egg yolks and poppy seeds. Sift together flour and baking soda. Add flour mixture to creamed mixture, alternating with sour cream. Begin and end with flour mixture. Combine beaten egg whites, almond and vanilla extracts, and cinnamon. Fold into batter. Pour mixture into prepared tube pan and bake 50 to 60 minutes or until cake tester comes out clean. Top immediately with lime syrup. Stir 1/2 cup fresh lime juice and 1/3 cup superfine sugar until sugar is dissolved. Pour over hot cake. Cool in pan. Serves 15–20

Shepherd's Pie

2 1/4 cups water

2 tablespoons finely chopped parsley

1 envelope Lipton Beefy Onion Recipe Soup Mix

1/2 cup each frozen cooked carrots and cooked peas

1/4 cup all purpose flour

1 quart hot mashed potatoes

1 quart cut-up cooked beef (about 1 1/2 pounds)

In large saucepan, bring 1 3/4 cups water to a boil. Stir in packaged soup mix, parsley and flour blended with remaining water. Bring to a boil, then simmer, stirring constantly until sauce is thickened, about 5 minutes. Stir in beef and vegetables. Turn into a 2 quart oblong baking dish. Top with potatoes and spread to completely cover beef mixture. Broil until golden. Makes about 6 servings.

Best Strawberry Punch

2 12-ounce cans frozen pink lemonade

2 1-litre bottles lemon lime soda, chilled

1 10-ounce frozen sliced strawberries

I have used this recipe for over twenty years and it's always a hit. Use it anytime you are serving a large group. Defrost lemonade and strawberries. Mix all of the above ingredients and add 2 cans cold water. Add ice ring or crushed ice or ice cubes. For a pretty mold, slightly freeze one half of the mold with water; add fresh fruit or edible flowers. Return to freezer for about one hour, then top with more water and freeze until solid. If you want to have colored ice, just add a few drops of food coloring. Another way to make your punch bowl attractive is to place a wreath of fresh flowers around the base, or just tie it with a pretty bow. One bowl serves 25 guests.

Friendship Tea

My sister used to make this mixture when I was a teenager. The same mix has been around the block a few times under different names. I prefer using Friendship Tea, because that is what taking tea is all about. This is also a good tea for children; they like the flavor and don't need to add sugar. It makes a nice hostess gift when packaged in a clear jar, wrapped in cellophane and tied with ribbon.

2 cups Tang instant drink
1 teaspoon ground cloves
1 cup sugar (optional)
1 cup instant tea
1/2 cup sweetened lemonade mix
1 teaspoon cinnamon

Mix all ingredients and stir using when needed, as any instant tea. Use two heaping teaspoons per cup, add boiling water.

Edible Flowers-The Ultimate Garnish

"How could such sweet and wholesome hours be
reckoned but in herbs and flowers?"

—Andrew Marvell

Decorating with fresh flowers adds beauty, fragrance and a sense of freshness to your tea table. Suggestions on how to use them to decorate just about any type of food include sprinkling them on top of cheese or garnishing sandwiches. It is a good idea to check a reliable source as to whether a flower is edible, and make sure that it has been grown free of pesticides. Your own garden grown flowers or those commercially raised for eating are the safest. Use only the flower blossoms or petals, never the leaves or stems. Here is a list of common edible flowers and what they taste or smell like:

Bachelor's Buttons (bland)   *Lilacs (lemon perfume)*
Dianthus (cloves)   *Nasturtiums (pepper, radish, watercress)*
Geranium (differs with variety)   *Pansies (sweet and mild)*
Johnny-Jump-Up (mild lettuce)   *Roses (floral)*
Lavender (floral, pungent)   *Violets (very floral)*

Chapter Ten

Forming a Tea Society

"Please bring your 'maddest' hat!"

—Alice in Wonderland

*I*t has been so much fun doing research on this topic. There are many different ways and ideas of organizing a society, whether it's for tea, book lovers, recipe collectors, dress-up, or whatever. Not one is right or wrong, just different, and is lead by special ladies, with their unique skills put in motion. A society is formed by a group of women with an idea and purpose in mind.

Why start a Tea Society?
- To be with your choice of friends, if for no other reason.
- To plan social functions together that you might not do otherwise.
- It is always more fun to do things with those you know.
- To have an excuse to dress up and do something "just for you."

Why belong to a Tea Society?
These groups offer many benefits. They help to motivate each other, to make new friends, and cultivate closer relationships with those who have similar interests. You will also have fun together, and share ideas with each other. Friends can gather to enjoy tea, crafts, reading, scrap booking, gardening, as well as other hobbies.

Who belongs to Tea Societies?
Tea Societies are made up of women with different goals. The make-up of the types of groups will vary. Some are ladies that prefer to go to tea. Some groups are for middle-aged and seasoned women such as the Red Hat Society, who do a variety of things, but always in their red hats and purple dresses. There are mother/daughter groups that gather together in different homes to teach the

young maidens homemaking skills and proper etiquette. One of my friends has a book group that meets monthly to exchange books and share stories they have read. The ideas are endless.

How does one start a Tea Group?

Ask a few of your friends, say eight to ten, if they would like to be a part of a social group. Most will no doubt be very excited to belong to such a regal circle. Of course there has to be an organizer, and that could be you. Gather your ladies together and work out some plans. Here are a few practical thoughts to help you get started.

How often do you want to meet?

- ❧ Does it always have to be at a tearoom or are there other options?

- ❧ Will there be dues?

- ❧ What will you name your group?

- ❧ Who will be the event chairman, if there is to be one?

- ❧ Will you have set rules, or be more casual, *qué sera sera*?

- ❧ Do you desire a dress code?

- ❧ Will there be a limited number of people who can join?

- ❧ Do we want to form a small group or keep expanding?

- ❧ Will you involve men in your group, or is it strictly for women?

Women's Mountain Bike and Tea Society (WOMBATS)

This is a ladies tea society that I found most interesting. It is a network of women of all ages and abilities who share a passion for pedaling in the dirt. These ladies go off-road for their bike riding experience.

After a couple of hours of off-road cycling it's time for a break. They find a lovely resting place under a large tree, sometimes with tables, and sometimes not. They pull up the ground if necessary and decorate it accordingly. Out come the lace tablecloth, teapot, teacups, and tidbits. These ladies come together in the outdoors for exercise, cycling, and to improve their riding skills.

Since 1984, Jacquie Phelan the founder of WOMBATS has been working hard to serve up a dish of flat tire fun to women. In her early years, Jacquie spent her time mastering miniature tea set ceremonies, reading Nancy Drew Mysteries, and catching frogs. For more information visit www.wombats.org

Victorian Tea Society

I had the pleasure of speaking with Joni Rick, President and Founder of The Victorian Tea Society in Murrieta, California. This group of adult ladies came into existence in 1998 because of their shared interest in Victoriana.

At the present time there are approximately 108 members of different ages. For various reasons some ladies must drop out, and others join. One unique detail is that they meet monthly in small groups of eight to ten, at different homes. Each member has an opportunity to experience being a hostess. She chooses the theme and menu and if the ladies should wear fun hats to the next gathering. They come together for tea, good conversation, laughter, and without rules or regulations. This is not to be a gossip session, or a time to be cliquish. It is a time to make everyone feel comfortable and welcome. The purpose of keeping the group small is that new relationships may be developed, and they can share openly their joys and sorrows.

At the in-home tea $10 per person is collected to cover expenses for food, fresh flowers, small gifts, and any other cost.

The Society has an annual Spring Tea, which is open to the public. This event gives all its members an opportunity to get to know those outside of their regular luncheon groups, and is designed strictly for a day of fun-filled activity and enjoyment. It also enables the public to see what The Victorian Tea Society is all about and to have a pleasurable day.

Luncheon groups stay together for one year, and if a member should want to change her group, this spring event is the time to do it. Oftentimes women have made such strong bonding with those of their immediate group they don't want to change.

The annual dues are $15 per person. This expense is to cover all running costs for the society, including a quarterly newsletter. The Victorian Tea Society is a non-profit organization and board members are strictly volunteers.

At Christmas, a hostess offers her home for an Open House Buffet Tea, which is held exclusively for society members. You don't have to have a large home to do this since people come and go on their schedule. How refreshing to be with those that have shared tea with you throughout the year.

*"A friend is a gift whose worth cannot be measured
except by the heart (unknown author)."*

The Ladies' Tea Guild

I found this information on the World Wide Web at www.glily.com. I am aware that not everyone has a computer, so I will be quoting some things from The Ladies' Tea Guild web site, and I think you will enjoy what is being done. To eliminate confusion about titles, The Ladies' Tea Guild is a branch of The Gilded Lily under the same auspice.

"The Ladies Tea Guild was established in the spring of 2001 with the intent of providing an oasis for women who have a passion for the past and/or a love of tea in all its dimensions. Our years of interest encompass 1800 through 1940. Our mission is to:

- ❧ Educate our members about the years 1800 through 1940 through our quarterly publication, The Gilded Lily.

- ❧ Research the customs, culture, and fashions of our time frame.

- ❧ Hostess unique and interesting social events where our members have the opportunity, should they so desire, to dress up in their favorite vintage or reproduction clothing.

"Through our events and social gatherings, create a community of like-minded women who understand the importance of sharing and helping one another; create endless opportunities for fun, laughter, and knowledge.

"While the Gilded Lily provides our members with a wealth of information, it is in our local chapters where the active fun begins. It is here that women wishing to mingle with others of like mind come together for a wide variety of interesting events and activities.

"Local chapters also hostess quarterly teas. Some of the events and activities are tea tasting, workshops and lectures. Members should plan to attend the quarterly teas dressed in appropriate attire so that the teas and socials are presented with a certain degree of elegance. While dressing in vintage fashion is not required, we do ask that a skirt or dress and a hat be considered. Of course, your biggest responsibility is to enjoy yourself and have fun!"

Trivia: The hand fan was very important during the Victorian era. The Victorian lady wore some of the most romantic costumes in history. Because they were hot and heavy almost every woman owned a fan, coordinating them to accessorize her wardrobe. The lady also needed the fan to cool herself in social gatherings.

The fan served to communicate one's wealth and social status, as well as to flirt. A fan placed across the eyes meant, "I love you." Placed on the right cheek it meant, "Yes" and on the left "No." The handle to the lips begged a kiss, dropping it meant friendship only. When placed behind the neck, it signified "Do not forget me." Maybe you would like to start a collection of fans as an interesting décor for your home.

The Red Hat Society

"There's Fun After Fifty" is the motto of the Red Hat Society. It was an honor for me to personally meet with the Exalted Queen Mother, Sue Ellen Cooper, the Founder of the Red hat Society in Fullerton, California at the hatquarters.

In 1997, Sue Ellen gave a copy of Jenny Joseph's poem, "Warning" and a bright red thrift store hat to her friend that was turning 50. The poem begins, "When I am old I shall wear purple, and a red hat that doesn't go and doesn't suit me." There were several friends turning 50 that year, and that was the beginning.

In April of 1998, Sue Ellen and her friends decided to find some purple outfits, put on their red hats and go out to tea. The magic that ensued resulted in the birth of the Red Hat Society.

This disorganization, (as is often referred to) happened purely as an accident. It was a fluke, and is growing by leaps and bounds. Actually, I think God was in it, and had a plan. At this writing there are 10,000 plus chapters of the Red Hat Society worldwide. Amazing!

I am the Queen Mother of a Red Hat Society chapter called, "The Charming Darlings." We are a small group of a bakers dozen. We have chosen to stay small. Most of our ladies prefer visiting a variety of tearooms, although we are flexible. Last Christmas some of us joined other chapters and we were in a small hometown parade. Now that's a hoot, riding in the back of a convertible waving the queenly wave with red-gloved hands. I would suggest everyone have that experience if possible. If you have ever wanted to be a celebrity, now is the time, as everyone talks to you and asks questions.

For those who have not yet reached fifty, take heart, someday you will. In the meantime, you will be a "lady in waiting." Isn't that a different connotation of the phrase? During your waiting period, don a pink hat, wear a lavender dress, and join your red hat seasoned friends. It is fun to have a mixed outing with the pinkies and let them see the frivolity the distinguished elders can have. Some pink hatters have started chapters of their own.

When a pink hatter reaches her fiftieth birthday, it is celebrated with "Reduation" ceremonies. In June of this year we had a pinkie, Susan Thompson, turn fifty and we surprised her during a tea outing. While a poem was being read she made her way to the platform to be crowned with a decorated red hat. It is as much fun for the red hatters witnessing such a coronation as it is for the one being crowned.

During my visit with Sue Ellen, I was most impressed with her casual demeanor. What else would I expect since the Red Hat Society has no rules, bylaws and claims to be disorganized. One of Sue Ellen's comments was a humble, "it's not about me, it's about women over fifty having fun, and this happens to be the venue for them to do that." For more information visit: www.redhatsociety.com

Well dear reader, I do hope this chapter has encouraged you to be the initiator to start your own society, whether it is for tea or some other group you choose to belong to.

"Share your life, and find the finest joy man can know. Do not be stingy with your heart. Get out of yourself into the lives of others, and new life will flow into you."

—Joseph Fort Newton

Chapter Eleven

How to Start a Prayer Tea

"The very breath of prayer sustains the Christian life"

—Carl F.H. Henry

So often women get together at restaurants, in their homes, and/or tearooms for fellowship. Sometimes even for shopping! Why not make your time more meaningful, and gather a group of six to ten like-minded ladies to meet on a monthly basis to pray for their husbands, children, their families, finances, country, attitudes, church, and any immediate needs.

Our group chose to meet on a weekday once a month. You may not be able to meet on a weekday for any number of reasons: employment, care of small children or other obligations. Perhaps you could try to schedule one Saturday morning a month for a Prayer Tea, or a weeknight that fits into your schedule. It would be best to have someone stay with the children for a couple of hours, or start a childcare co-op, then you can reciprocate at another time.

Our gathering of ladies meets from 9:00 to 11:00 A.M. on the first Monday of each month. It is beneficial for each lady to take a turn in her home to hostess a Prayer Tea. Each one has her own special gifts that the Lord has given her, and it gives her the opportunity to practice hospitality.

For the first 30 to 45 minutes we have tea with scones, or whatever other sweets the hostess has prepared for that day. This is a special time to unwind and go over happenings of the past month with each other. At 9:45 we settle down with our Bibles and prayer journals. The hostess opens in prayer and leads in a short devotional.

We take prayer requests and go over any answered prayer from our last gathering. This time is very personal. We don't share outside our group unless it is an urgent request and have been given permission to do so. At this time each lady takes her turn in praying for the person on her right and anything else that might be pressing on her heart. She may want to give praises to God for answered prayer, who He is, and all that He does for each one of us. These prayer requests are also noted in our journals so that we hold our sisters up in prayer during our time apart. We try to limit this time to fifteen minutes, as there is still much to cover.

Spending time together in fellowship encourages women to pray aloud. Some have never been exposed to it before. They need to be encouraged that the words they say aren't the important part, they are talking to God, not trying to impress others with eloquent speech.

Fellowship does not simply mean social relations, but that we are to be partakers of His word and share our joys with others in Christ. Pastor John Mac Arthur says, "Scripture should permeate every aspect of the believer's life and control every thought, word and deed."

Be prepared for the schemes of Satan. He doesn't want these prayer meetings to go on, and will try to distract you. He wants your mind to drift and your heart to be troubled, so we must zoom in more intently on the task before us. Be alert on the times you are to meet and stay focused, not allowing the enemy to win victory over your time in the Word.

Scripture also tells us we are to pray without ceasing, and with the expectation of seeing results. We are to devote ourselves to prayer, which means making time for listening to the Father as well as for talking to Him. God hears, God answers.

When we are finished with prayer requests, we go to the next portion of our prayer time.

The method, which we have set up for our group, is ACTS: Adoration, Confession, Thanksgiving and Supplication. Each lady prays as the Spirit moves her; it is not necessary that each one pray, as long as everything is covered. Sometimes the hostess prays the entire formula.

Adoration: Should be the easy part, as there are so many reasons to praise God. The Psalms are a good place to start. Praise Him for one or more of His attributes: love, compassion, mercy, grace, holiness, and much more. It is suggested to do a word study of all His attributes during your personal time of study. Put them in alphabetical order, and then memorize them for future reference.

Confession: A time for you to come before the throne of grace and confess your sins to Him, ask for His forgiveness, and be cleansed. Ask the Holy Spirit to search your heart and reveal any areas of unconfessed sin in your own private thoughts. There is no need to share your personal sin in public; God knows. It is so refreshing to know that you can be cleansed as white as snow, and start with a clean slate. Thank Him for His forgiveness.

Thanksgiving: "Devote yourselves to prayer, keeping alert in it with an attitude of thanksgiving" (Colossians 4:2). Thank Him for answered prayer, for good health, for His Word, promises, faithfulness and whatever else is on your heart.

Supplication: Or petition is a time for us to bring others before our God, as well as any of our own personal needs. Here are some suggestions, not necessarily in any order: salvation of family members and friends, our government, pastor, church elders, other believers, and world affairs; for personal concerns, our own growth in Christ, growth in wisdom, spiritual insight, a passion to obey God, and relationship with others. "Earnestly seek God and make your supplication to the Almighty" (Job 8:5).

For our prayer journals, most use the easy to find small 5 x 7 cloth covered notebook with lined paper inside. We use these only with our prayer group, and don't mix them with other personal journals. When one is filled, start another. They are wonderful to review at a later time and see what the Lord has done in each of our lives.

When it's my time to hostess the Prayer Tea, I like to use Matthew 6:33 as our opening verse. "But seek first His kingdom, and His righteousness, and all these things shall be added to you." If we don't seek Him first, what are we doing here? If Jesus is truly the Lord of our life and we have given Him complete control, then that must mean we can trust Him with everything. That means not withholding one iota from Him. He knows our thoughts and wants us to tell Him about it. God is seeking intimacy with us. What sweet rewards come from opening your all to Him, as He gives direction for our lives.

I recommend not taking time to do dishes while your guests are there. Just rinse the dishes, fill your sink with hot soapy water and let everything soak. Over a two-hour period dishes are clean, with a quick swipe of the dishcloth, rinse and dry, *voilá* you're done.

What an enriching time it is to be able to pray with sisters in the Lord. It knits hearts together, and you will discover a closer relationship with Him that is indescribable. We really do become bonded, kindred spirits in Jesus.

Pastor Charles Stanley says, "Prayer is so simple. Truly, it is the act of communicating openly with God. It is a matter of giving time to the Father to let Him do in your life what He chooses to do." Amen to that.

The Teacup Story

*"Behold, like the clay in the potter's hand,
so are you in my hand.".*

—Jeremiah 18:6b

*I*would like to leave you with this inspiring little story about "The Teacup,"
by an unknown author.

*There was a couple that used to go to England to shop in the beautiful stores.
They both liked antiques and pottery, especially teacups. This was their
twenty-fifth wedding anniversary. One day in a beautiful shop they saw an
exquisite teacup. They asked the clerk, "May we see that? We've never seen
one quite so lovely."*

*As the lady handed it to them, suddenly the teacup spoke. "You don't under-
stand," it said. "I haven't always been a teacup. There was a time when I was
red, and I was clay. My master took me and rolled me and patted me over
and over, and I yelled out, 'let me alone,' but he only smiled and said, 'Not
yet.' Then I was placed on a spinning wheel and suddenly spun around, and
around, and around. 'Stop it! I'm getting dizzy!' I screamed.*

*"But the master only nodded and said, 'Not yet.' Then he put me in the oven.
I never felt such heat. I wondered why he wanted to burn me, and I yelled
and knocked at the door. I could see him through the opening, and I could read
his lips, as he shook his head, 'Not yet.'*

*"Finally the door opened, he put me on a shelf, and I began to cool. 'There,
that's better,' I said. And he brushed, and painted me all over. The fumes were
horrible. I thought I would gag. 'Stop it, stop it!' I cried. He only nodded, 'Not
yet.' Then suddenly he put me back into the oven, not like the first one. This
was twice as hot, and I knew I would suffocate. I begged. I pleaded.*

I screamed. I cried. All the time I could see him through the opening nodding his head saying, 'Not yet.'

"Then I knew there wasn't any hope. I would never make it. I was ready to give up. But the door opened, and he took me out and placed me on a shelf. One hour later he handed me a mirror and said, 'Look at yourself.' And I did. I said, 'That's not me, that couldn't be me. It's beautiful. I'm beautiful.'

"'I want you to remember, then,' he said, 'I know it hurts to be rolled and patted, but if I had left you alone, you'd have dried up. I know it made you dizzy to spin around on the wheel, but if I had stopped, you would have crumbled. I knew it hurt, and was hot and disagreeable in the oven, but if I hadn't put you there, you would have cracked.

"'I know the fumes were bad when I brushed and painted you all over, but if I hadn't done that, you never would have hardened; you would not have had any color in your life. And if I hadn't put you back in that second oven, you wouldn't survive for very long because the hardness would not have held. Now you are a finished product. You are what I had in mind when I first began with you.'"

Moral: God knows what He is doing for all of us. He is the Potter, and we are His clay. He will mold us and make us, so that we may be made into a flawless piece of work to fulfill His good, pleasing, and perfect will.

This story has a personal meaning to me as I imagine myself as the teacup, and reminds me of how patient the Master Potter has been. He literally takes me into His hands and continues to mold and transform me into His image. As it says in 2 Corinthians 5:17, "Therefore if any man is in Christ, he is a new creature; the old things passed away; behold, new things have come."